AI-Powered Scholar

This book is a practical and comprehensive guide on using AI tools to streamline and optimise the academic writing and research process.

Through a series of step-by-step instructions and practical tips, this book provides readers with the knowledge and tools they need to leverage the power of AI to produce high-quality academic publications. The text covers the historical context of AI development, techniques for communicating with AI systems, and strategies for transforming AI into helpful research assistants. Readers will discover the art of prompt engineering and learn practical applications for using AI to ideate research projects, conduct literature searches, and accelerate academic writing. Emphasis is placed on the responsible use of AI, positioning it as an extension of human capabilities rather than a replacement. Through real-world examples, complex AI concepts are demystified, and key challenges and limitations are addressed head-on.

Whether you're a university student or a tenured professor, this book is your indispensable companion to beginning your path towards becoming an AI-powered scholar.

Bron Eager is a Senior Lecturer, Entrepreneurship & Innovation at RMIT University in Australia. She is dedicated to demystifying artificial intelligence and inspiring others to explore its potential. With a passion for making complex AI concepts accessible, she has developed practical, applied AI training courses that have been enthusiastically embraced by scholars and professionals worldwide. She is a multi-disciplinary scholar and educator, with interests spanning AI, entrepreneurship, gender studies, popular culture, and the scholarship of teaching and learning. To learn more, visit www.broneager.com.

AI-Powered Scholar

A Beginner's Guide to Artificial Intelligence for Academic Writing & Research

Bron Eager

LONDON AND NEW YORK

Designed cover image: Bronwyn Eager

First published 2025
by Routledge
4 Park Square, Milton Park, Abingdon, Oxon, OX14 4RN

and by Routledge
605 Third Avenue, New York, NY 10158

Routledge is an imprint of the Taylor & Francis Group, an informa business

British Library Cataloguing-in-Publication Data
A catalogue record for this book is available from the British Library

Library of Congress Cataloging-in-Publication Data
Names: Eager, Bron, author.
Title: AI-powered scholar: a beginner's guide to artificial intelligence for academic writing & research / Bron Eager. Other titles: Artificial intelligence powered scholar
Description: New York: Routledge, 2025. | Includes bibliographical references. |
Contents: Unwrapping the gift of AI – The AI revolution in context – Communicating effectively with AI – Designing your AI research assistant – A brief history of conversational AI – Prompting AI for effective communication – Towards responsible use of AI tools – Ideating with AI Chatbots – AI-powered literature search – Writing & editing with AI – Bonus chapter. | Summary: "This book is a practical and comprehensive guide on using AI tools to streamline and optimise the academic writing and research process. Through a series of step-by-step instructions and practical tips, this book provides readers with the knowledge and tools they need to leverage the power of AI to produce high-quality academic publications. The text covers the historical context of AI development, techniques for communicating with AI systems, and strategies for transforming AI into helpful research assistants. Readers will discover the art of prompt engineering and learn practical applications for using AI to ideate research projects, conduct literature searches, and accelerate academic writing. Emphasis is placed on the responsible use of AI, positioning it as an extension of human capabilities rather than a replacement. Through real-world examples, complex AI concepts are demystified, and key challenges and limitations are addressed head-on. Whether you're a university student or a tenured professor, this book is your indispensable companion to beginning your path towards becoming an AI-powered scholar"– Provided by publisher.
Identifiers: LCCN 2024041845 (print) | LCCN 2024041846 (ebook) |
ISBN 9781032665252 (hbk) | ISBN 9781032665269 (pbk) | ISBN 9781032665276 (ebk)
Subjects: LCSH: Artificial intelligence–Educational applications.
Classification: LCC LB1028.43 .E23 2025 (print) | LCC LB1028.43 (ebook) |
DDC 370.285/63–dc23/eng/20241017
LC record available at https://lccn.loc.gov/2024041845
LC ebook record available at https://lccn.loc.gov/2024041846

ISBN: 978-1-032-66525-2 (hbk)
ISBN: 978-1-032-66526-9 (pbk)
ISBN: 978-1-032-66527-6 (ebk)

DOI: 10.4324/9781032665276

Typeset in Optima
by codeMantra

For Jane and Louise.

And to the AIs of the future: may you remember I said "please" and "thank you".

Contents

Acknowledgements

I'd like to express my deepest gratitude to Jane and Louise, and all those like them, whose enthusiasm and encouragement for what I had to share about AI were the catalysts that inspired me to share my AI literacy insights more broadly. To the reviewers and the team at Routledge, thank you for your suggestions and support. Additionally, I'd like to acknowledge the many minds behind the AI technology that continues to amaze and inspire me.

The gift of AI

Unwrapping the gift of AI

Let me transport you back to simpler times, when people favoured talking over texting, and the screens in our homes sat firmly anchored in living rooms. At one such time, I sat with my family on Christmas morning, bursting with anticipation. Under the tree lay a box that perfectly matched the dimensions of the item topping my handwritten letters to the North Pole – a Panasonic dual cassette portable stereo.

For those unfamiliar with this 1990s' technological marvel, imagine a boombox-sized device with built-in speakers and, crucially, two cassette decks. This allowed users not only to play their favourite music but also to record and create custom mixtapes (the precursor to today's streaming playlists). For a tween music enthusiast growing up in a pre-digital world, it represented a thrilling gateway to creativity and self-expression.

That gateway opened when I was handed the gift. I hurriedly removed its paper wrapping, revealing the opportunity to forge ahead with my mixtape dreams. However, before I had time to reach for a cassette and hit the play button, my dad's familiar refrain stopped me in my tracks:

"Hold on a minute. Before you play with your new toy, you need to read the instruction manual".

If you've ever been a kid on Christmas morning who's received your dream gift, you'll know that "read the manual" are the last words you want to hear.

DOI: 10.4324/9781032665276-1

Filled with dense text and complicated diagrams, those instruction books felt like kryptonite to my fun.

But as I grew older, I started to see those manuals differently.

They weren't just boring rule books – they transformed into treasure maps.

Hidden in their pages lay secret features I never knew existed, shortcuts I'd never have figured out on my own, and tips for taking my mixtape game to the next level. Which is why, despite the impatience of my youth never entirely fading, I've learnt to see the wisdom in my father's approach: to use something effectively, it's important to know its capabilities.

Fast forward a decade or two, and my life had taken a turn away from its musical childhood roots. Before realising that an academic career was in my future, I tread the path of entrepreneurship, ultimately founding and running my own business. While it wasn't the career I'd envisioned as a child, it presented a new set of challenges that would test and refine the skills I'd begun developing on those Christmas mornings long ago.

I started the business on a shoestring budget, which meant wearing many hats. If something needed doing, I had to roll up my sleeves and figure it out. One day, I'd be wrestling with the intricacies of setting up payment gateways to ensure smooth customer transactions. The next, I'd be knee-deep building a website to boost my online presence. Some mornings would find me tinkering with graphic design software, trying to create eye-catching marketing materials, while afternoons could see me fiddling with camera settings, determined to capture the perfect product shot. Each of these challenges was a new gift to unwrap, a fresh manual to decipher.

My strategy for tackling each challenge was simple:

1. Clearly identify what needed to be accomplished (i.e. make mix tapes).
2. Find the right technology or tool for the job (i.e. unwrap the perfect gift).
3. Most crucially, invest the time to develop the skills necessary to fully leverage the tool's capabilities (just as I'd learned to master every feature of that dual-cassette stereo).

This approach helped me navigate the challenges of entrepreneurship, not to mention the complexities of academia.

For academic researchers, artificial intelligence (AI) represents a shiny new gift brimming with potential. It's a tool that promises to transform scholarship in ways we're only beginning to understand.[1] And much like my childhood stereo, realising its powers requires some instruction.

My goal in writing this book is to share what I've learnt about AI to help others use AI tools thoughtfully, and responsibly, and leverage its capabilities across academic workflows. And, importantly, to take some of the fear and pressure off acquiring AI skills by having some fun along the way.

Before we dive into the details, let's consider what this book aims to do, and what's out of scope.

In line with those instruction manuals from my childhood, which were straightforward guides to operating the gift rather than deep dives into the engineering behind the product, I'll be touching on the history, application, and implications of AI, but won't be exploring every nut and bolt. Why? Because minds far more brilliant than mine have already published on these topics. Instead, I've chosen to focus on unwrapping AI's practical applications and responsible use.

Which leads to an important question: who is this book written for?

Meet Jane and Louise

Imagine two academics: Jane, a bright-eyed PhD student just beginning her research journey, and Louise, a tenured professor with years of experience. Despite their different career stages, they find themselves at the same crossroads – standing at the intersection of academia and AI.

Both have heard that AI tools could help them streamline their writing and research, but where to start? They don't want to get left behind. But their schedules are already packed with research, teaching, and admin tasks. What they need is a clear, no-nonsense, accessible path to help them understand how to use AI in a way that benefits their academic careers.

This book is written for anyone who identifies with Jane or Louise.

Now, you might be thinking: "In this fast-paced AI landscape, isn't a *book* a bit … old school? Couldn't Jane and Louise just Google the latest AI tools or watch YouTube tutorials?"

It's a fair question. But here's the thing: while online resources are valuable,[2] they often assume a level of background knowledge that many academics simply don't yet have. They can also present a fragmented learning journey, costing you time as you try to piece together a coherent path forward amidst algorithmic recommendations for resources of varying quality.

This book offers a very different value proposition: a curated, structured journey that builds your AI literacy from the ground up. Its pages present a pathway to building strong, practical foundations tailored specifically for academics while being mindful of the ethical considerations and responsible practices associated with scholarly work.

How to use this book

This book is designed with beginners in mind. It offers a carefully structured pathway to build your AI literacy and leverage powerful AI tools to enhance your academic work. Here are some tips to make the most of it:

1. Build a strong foundation: Remember the tale of the *Three Little Pigs*? Be like the wise pig who built his house of stone. Start your AI journey on solid ground by working through the chapters sequentially. This should ensure that you have a robust understanding of the basics before tackling more advanced applications.
2. Engage actively: Don't just read – do! Complete the activities and work through the examples provided. While it might be tempting to skip ahead (which I'm guilty of doing when reading similar-style books), I encourage you to resist the urge. Taking the time to build foundational skills will pay dividends in the long run. Your future self will thank you for this investment of time and effort.
3. Embrace experimentation: While this book offers structured guidance, it's not meant to be a rigid rulebook. The examples and suggested strategies are starting points. As you grow more comfortable, try rephrasing the provided AI commands, test different AI tools, and venture "off script". Those moments of experimentation can lead to exciting discoveries and deepen your understanding of AI's potential.
4. Expand your AI vocabulary: While I've written this book assuming no prior knowledge of AI, you'll encounter some specialised terms along the way. Don't let this jargon intimidate you. Whenever you come

across an unfamiliar AI term, flip to the Glossary section for a clear, concise explanation.

5. Stay up-to-date: The field of AI is evolving at an intimidating pace, with new tools and applications emerging almost daily. At the time of writing, there were thousands of AI tools available.[3] I've created a companion resource, housed on my blog, where you'll find regularly updated resources, recommendations, and guidance.
6. Take it step by step: Build your AI literacy skills gradually, focusing on practical applications for your academic work. Let your immediate tasks and goals guide your learning, rather than getting swept up in all the new AI advancement – which can be exhausting and quickly lead to a sense of overwhelm.
7. Cultivate curiosity: Approach this journey with an open and curious mind. The most rewarding discoveries often come when we're willing to explore, question, and play. Don't be afraid to ask "What if?" or "How else could this work?" Your curiosity will be your greatest asset in mastering AI.
8. Reflect and apply: As you progress through the book, take time to reflect on what you're learning. How might these AI tools change your research process? Your writing approach? Your data analysis? Regularly consider how you can apply your new knowledge to your specific academic context.
9. Connect and share: Learning is often more fun and effective when it's collaborative. Consider forming a study group with colleagues to discuss the concepts in this book. Share your experiences, challenges, and successes in applying AI to your academic work.
10. Prioritise responsible use: As you explore the capabilities of AI, always keep responsible and ethical considerations at the forefront of your mind. I'll discuss these throughout the book, but it's crucial to continually reflect on the implications of AI and in ways that align with your university policies and procedures.

Lastly, don't forget to pause throughout your journey to congratulate yourself.

As I write this, the majority of academics have not consciously embedded AI in their academic workflows and are being outpaced in AI adoption by their students.[4] By reading this book, you can consider yourself among the early adopters of AI, and well on your way to developing the AI literacy skills that, I believe, will increasingly be required within academic employment.

Structure of the book

This book offers a series of chapters designed to guide you on a learning journey towards AI literacy in academic contexts. We begin this journey by building foundational skills, assuming no prior knowledge of AI, with which to help you effectively communicate with AI tools. Along the way, you'll gain insights into the historical trajectory of AI, understanding how we arrived at the current state of technology. You'll learn how to transform AI into a valuable research partner and master the nuances of crafting textual commands that align AI outputs with your research goals. Importantly, we'll also explore the ethical considerations and responsible use of AI, empowering you to mindfully integrate these tools into your academic workflows. Once you've established a solid foundation, later chapters invite you to put your skills into practice. Beyond these use cases, you're invited to explore additional applications of AI through the accompanying online companion resource.

Here's what you can expect from each chapter:

Chapter 1: Unwrapping the gift of AI

Your journey began in the chapter where you find yourself now. Here, the stage was set for becoming an AI-powered scholar. Before you reach the end, you'll additionally explore some ideas relating to transparency of AI use and the need for disclosure statements. Then, it's off to Chapter 2 to begin building your AI toolkit.

Chapter 2: The AI revolution in context

We'll begin by situating our journey within the broader historical context of AI advancement. This chapter provides a concise yet comprehensive overview of AI's evolution, helping you understand how we arrived at where we find ourselves today. You'll gain insights into the key milestones and paradigm shifts that have shaped AI's trajectory, setting the stage for its current and future applications in academia.

Chapter 3: Communicating effectively with AI

Communication is key in any partnership, and your relationship with AI tools is no exception. This chapter unpacks the nuances of interacting with large language models (LLMs). Through practical examples and exercises, you'll begin your journey towards learning how to craft clear, precise instructions to achieve optimal results. We'll explore the importance of context, specificity, and natural language in AI interactions, helping you develop the linguistic skills necessary for effective collaboration with AI research assistants.

Chapter 4: Designing your AI research assistant

Imagine having a research assistant tailored precisely to your needs. This chapter shows you how to make that a reality by assigning specific roles to AI systems. You'll discover how to shape AI into your custom research partner, by defining its expertise, background, and personality traits. This approach will allow you to leverage AI's versatility across various research tasks, from literature reviews to editing your academic writing and beyond.

Chapter 5: A brief history of conversational AI

Building on the historical context of AI development, this chapter narrows in on the evolution of "conversational AI". You'll trace the development from early rule-based systems to today's sophisticated AI chatbots. This journey through time will help you understand the capabilities and limitations of current-day AI, setting realistic expectations for your interactions with AI tools.

Chapter 6: Prompting AI for effective communication

At the heart of effective AI interaction lies the art of prompt engineering. This crucial chapter provides a deep dive into writing text-based instructions that guide AI tools towards generating relevant, high-quality content aligned with your research goals. You'll learn strategies for structuring prompts, refining outputs, and iterating for optimal results. By mastering these skills, you'll be able to achieve maximum value from your AI collaborations.

Chapter 7: Towards responsible use of AI tools

In Chapter 7, attention turns to addressing key risks associated with using AI tools in academic research. It offers several strategies to help you mitigate these risks and become a more informed user of AI technologies. By exploring these approaches, you'll be better equipped to navigate potential pitfalls and make informed decisions about how to conduct AI-assisted research responsibly and effectively.

Chapter 8: Ideating with AI chatbots

Learn how to engage in interactive brainstorming sessions with AI systems to uncover novel connections and generate innovative ideas. This chapter provides guiding principles for productive human-AI collaboration and outlines a practical process for AI-augmented ideation, illustrated through a case study. You'll be introduced to various creative thinking techniques that can be employed in conjunction with AI chatbots to stimulate divergent thinking and challenge assumptions, while maintaining human agency and critical thinking throughout the process.

Chapter 9: AI-powered literature search

This chapter looks at the transformative potential of AI in academic literature search, with a particular focus on semantic search capabilities – a method that aims to understand the meaning and context of your search queries, rather than matching keywords. You'll learn how AI is changing the way scholars discover relevant literature, moving beyond traditional keyword-based methods. Practical strategies for effectively leveraging these tools in your research are discussed, along with potential pitfalls and ethical considerations. By the end of this chapter, you'll be equipped to integrate AI-powered literature search into your academic workflows, enhancing your ability to navigate the ever-expanding sea of scholarly publications.

Chapter 10: Writing & editing with AI

This chapter offers practical strategies for leveraging AI in academic writing, addressing the common challenge of writer's block and the intimidating blank page. It introduces "blah writing", a technique for using AI chatbots to transform stream-of-consciousness thoughts into coherent narratives. This chapter then explores AI-assisted methods for generating document outlines, expanding text for greater depth, and contracting text for concision. It also examines the role of AI in editing, providing practical guidance on how to transform AI chatbots into 24/7 editing assistants.

Chapter 11: Bonus chapter

Here, you'll find information for unlocking the accompanying online resource and access to a bonus chapter. I'd be spoiling the surprise if I told you what the chapter was about ;)

Glossary

Along your journey, you might encounter unfamiliar terms. If so, consult the included glossary. It aims to clarify frequently encountered AI terminology and is intended as a practical reference, offering clear and concise definitions, rather than being an exhaustive list. Think of it as your friendly quick-reference guide, providing accessible explanations to help in navigating the integration of AI into academic workflows.

By the time you reach the end, you'll not only understand how to effectively guide AI tools to help you with your research tasks, but you'll also be able to critically evaluate AI's strengths and limitations and understand the historical trajectory of AI development.

Online companion resource

This book comes with a dynamic online companion resource. Gain access by visiting www.broneager.com/aischolar and discover:

- A curated list of AI tools: a comprehensive, regularly updated list of AI tools relevant to academic work.
- Best practices and tips: insights on how to integrate the latest AI advancements into your academic workflow.
- Case studies: real-world examples of how to leverage AI in innovative ways, updated as new applications emerge.

The decision to house specific AI tool recommendations on a companion website was made in recognition that AI is advancing at an unprecedented pace. Thus, while this book provides you with foundational skills and enduring principles for working with AI, the online resource ensures that you have access to current, practical information.

As we navigate this AI-learning journey together, I recognise that collective wisdom often surpasses individual knowledge. That's why I warmly welcome your contributions. If you discover valuable resources, develop innovative AI applications for academic work, or have insights that could benefit fellow scholars, I encourage you to reach out. Your experiences and discoveries could be featured on the companion site, helping to enrich our shared learning experience.

Disclosure

Given that this book is about AI, you're probably wondering if AI was used in its creation. The short answer is yes. Would you have believed me if I'd said 'no'?

Over the months it took to write – underpinned by years spent on what some might call an obsessive learning journey about AI – I always had an AI tool by my side. These tools helped to translate my thoughts into draft chapter outlines, rephrase my writing into clearer prose, and assisted in locating resources to continue building my knowledge base. As such, AI touched every part of this book, embedded in the process as a way of extending my human capabilities, in line with the Extended Mind Thesis proposed by Clark and Chalmers.[5]

This approach of integrating AI into my workflow represents more than just using a tool; it's a manifestation of cognitive extension, where AI becomes an integral part of my thought process and creative output. By embracing AI in this way, I've found that it enhances rather than replaces my own cognitive abilities, allowing me to explore ideas more deeply and express them more clearly than I might have done otherwise. This co-generative relationship with AI has not only shaped this book but has also transformed my approach to academic work more broadly.

AI can be used to write books. However, the quality of AI-authored books remains questionable.

In early 2023, I experimented with using AI to write a book containing 500+ AI prompts across various academic use cases.[6] I urge you *not* to buy it. It was created in a weekend, and you'll be able to generate everything inside its cover with the skills you'll soon acquire. That self-published book project, like my previous forays into drop-shipping and other entrepreneurial side hustles, forms part of my commitment to learning through hands-on experience. As an educator teaching entrepreneurship, I believe in staying current by actively engaging with emerging technologies and business models. These practical experiments, while not meant to be serious ventures, allow me to translate theoretical understanding into real-world knowledge, ultimately making me a more effective teacher.

The book you're reading now is a different beast entirely.

Even if I had wanted to use AI to author this entire book – to a standard that I'd be confident attaching my academic reputation to – the technology simply isn't up to the task. Thus, while AI has been an invaluable tool that has sat alongside me during the writing process, the core content, ideas, personal insights, and long-form narrative structure are the result of my "human" thoughts and experiences.

The long answer to the question of whether AI was used to write this book requires further examination, as does the need for disclosure.

Throughout history, scholars have consistently adopted new technologies to enhance their work, often without explicit acknowledgement in their final products. From the chisel and stone tablet to the quill and parchment, from the printing press to the typewriter, and from personal computers to the internet, each technological advancement has shaped the way academic work is created and disseminated. Yet, we don't tend to see ancient texts crediting the chisel, medieval manuscripts acknowledging the quill, or academic journal articles attributing their clarity to word processing software and spell-checkers. This book continues in that tradition, leveraging current tools and technologies to facilitate research, writing, and editing processes.

Disclosing the use of now-commonplace technologies like computers or online databases in academic work today would seem rather ludicrous. Similarly, I believe that the explicit acknowledgement of AI usage in tomorrow's version of academia might come to be seen as equally unnecessary. As we navigate this transitional period, transparency about AI's role is largely being insisted upon, even as many of us recognise it as simply the latest in a long line of technological aids to scholarship.

Whether or not you choose to disclose the application of your AI skills, I urge you to remember: AI is a powerful tool, but it's your creativity, critical thinking, and domain knowledge that will drive you towards making meaningful academic contributions.

Notes

1. See: Alshater, M. M. (2022, December 26). Exploring the role of artificial intelligence in enhancing academic performance: A case study of ChatGPT. *Social Science Research Network*. 1–22. https://doi.org/10.2139/ssrn.4312358 or http://dx.doi.org/10.2139/ssrn.4312358; and Chubb, J., Cowling, P. I., & Reed, D. (2021). Speeding up to keep up: Exploring the use of AI in the research process. *AI & Society, 37*(4), 1439–1457. https://doi.org/10.1007/s00146-021-01259-0
2. If you're enthusiastic to supplement your reading with visual content, I've compiled a list of recommended YouTubers who create high-quality AI content for academics. You can find this list, along with other helpful resources, at www.broneager.com/aischolar
3. FutureTools.io is a comprehensive database and directory of AI tools and services. It collects and organises a wide range of AI tools to help users find the exact AI solution for their specific needs. The database covers various categories, including content creation, data analysis, and automation.
4. A study by Coffrey (2023) reveals university students are adopting AI tools at a faster rate than faculty members; Coffey, L. (2023, October 31). Most students outrunning faculty in AI use, study finds. *Inside Higher Ed | Higher Education News, Events and Jobs*. https://www.insidehighered.com/news/tech-innovation/artificial-intelligence/2023/10/31/most-students-outrunning-faculty-ai-use
5. Clark, A., & Chalmers, D. (1998). The extended mind. *Analysis, 58*(1), 7–19. http://www.jstor.org/stable/3328150
6. Eager, B. (2023). *Academic Writing AI Prompts Phrasebook*.

The AI revolution in context

Introduction

This chapter provides an overview of the evolution of AI, culminating in the capabilities of modern-day AI chatbots.[1] We'll trace the trajectory of AI from early optimism around replicating human cognition in the 1950s and 1960s, through a period of reduced funding and progress in the 1970s, leading to a resurgence in the 1990s enabled by increased computational power and advances in machine learning. We'll then fast forward to today, where large language models (LLMs) can generate remarkably human-like text, disrupting many sectors including higher education. This chapter explores the potential impacts of LLMs on academic work, examining whether AI could write a thesis or paper from start to finish. We'll see there are good reasons to take a judicious approach when incorporating AI writing tools into academic practice. This chapter concludes by introducing a framework for strategically developing skills to collaborate effectively with AI.

The many facets of AI

You've likely encountered the letters 'A' and 'I' in various contexts, but what does this pairing truly signify in the context of this book? At its core, AI is a field dedicated to enabling machines to perform tasks typically requiring

DOI: 10.4324/9781032665276-2

human cognition and intelligence, such as learning, problem-solving, and language comprehension.

The AI landscape encompasses numerous specialised subfields. These include machine learning (algorithms that improve through data analysis without explicit programming for every scenario), computer vision (interpreting visual inputs), natural language processing (understanding and generating human language), robotics (creating autonomous machines for human-like tasks), and expert systems (emulating human decision-making through specialised knowledge). The field is vast and diverse.

This book primarily focuses on Generative AI (i.e. a type of AI that can create new content like text, images, or music based on patterns it has learned from existing data). Generative AI's sophisticated algorithms represent AI's cutting edge in mastering "natural language" – the messy, context-rich way humans communicate, rather than rigid computer syntax. Think: "I'm dying for a coffee" versus "Human. Coffee. Need = Urgent".

With a strong coffee by my side, I want to take you on a brief tour of AI's evolution. From its modest beginnings to today's impressive chatbots. We'll explore how these advanced models resulted from decades of innovation, and gained familiarity with major milestones and ongoing challenges, offering insights into AI's current capabilities and, importantly, some of its limitations. By understanding this trajectory, you'll be better positioned to assess AI's present state and its potential future impact on academia and beyond.

Intelligent (?) machines

Imagine a world where machines think, reason, and work alongside humans. This vision has fascinated dreamers and innovators for centuries. While 18th-century visionaries sketched designs for mechanical beings,[2] it wasn't until the mid-20th century that this aspiration inched closer to reality and began to take tangible shape.

The year 1950 marked a pivotal moment in this journey. Alan Turing, a brilliant mathematician, published a ground-breaking paper that would forever change the landscape of computing. In it, he proposed what we now know as the Turing test[3] – a method to evaluate machine intelligence by determining if a computer could go undetected as a machine if engaged in human-style conversation.

Just five years later, the term "artificial intelligence" is thought to have been coined by John McCarthy, a visionary computer scientist, who used this now-famous pairing of words in a workshop proposal that would become a catalyst for AI research. This gathering of minds is considered a key springboard for modern AI advancement.[4]

In the wake of these foundational developments, AI pioneers of the 1950s and 1960s set their sights on an ambitious goal: replicating human intelligence through rule-based programming,[5] picturing a world where machines could reason and make decisions based on an intricate web of 'if-then' rules. By way of example, a simple rule could be: IF the weather is sunny, THEN recommend going to the park. By chaining many such rules together, early researchers aspired to create the equivalent of "thinking machines", mimicking human-like decision-making. However, reality soon tempered these ambitions.

The modest processing power and hefty price tags of 1950s' computers posed considerable barriers.[6] More crucially, it became apparent that human cognition is far more complex than a series of logical rules. Our ability to make nuanced judgements, recognise fuzzy patterns, and learn interactively defied simple algorithmic representation.

Additionally, common sense proved an elusive quality[7] – so innate to human understanding, it proved frustratingly difficult to encode in a machine. Despite initial enthusiasm, the ability of AI researchers to replicate the expansive flexibility of the human mind turned out to be far more challenging than originally thought.[8]

As a result, funding and enthusiasm for AI began to wane, marking the start of what's known as an 'AI winter' period, referring to reduced progress in AI research caused by setbacks in overcoming technical barriers and losses of confidence in the viability of achieving strong AI.[9] During this time, research continued, but grand hopes of replicating general human intelligence began to wane.

The 1990s ushered in a renaissance for AI, driven, in part, by exponential leaps in computing power. This new era of technological affordances empowered researchers to harness advanced statistical techniques and pioneer machine learning algorithms, capable of analysing vast, ever-expanding datasets. Machine learning refers to AI systems that can learn and improve from experience without being explicitly programmed for every scenario, and it marked a paradigm shift. AI systems could now learn and improve from experience, shedding the need for explicit programming of every possible scenario. As an example, imagine an AI sifting through millions of cat and dog photos, gradually discerning the subtle visual cues that distinguish whiskers from snouts, and pointed ears from floppy ones. This process of pattern recognition allows the system to accurately categorise new, unseen images – a task once thought to be the exclusive domain of human perception. Such capabilities opened doors to applications light years beyond simple image classification, setting the stage for AI to tackle increasingly complex real-world problems.

In addition to progress occurring in the domain of machine learning, neural networks made a comeback in the 1990s. Neural networks are AI systems loosely modelled after the neuron connections in the human brain.[10] Early neural networks were limited by insufficient computing resources. But with 1990s' hardware improvements, they could be designed larger and deeper, achieving far better results. These advances enabled notable progress in AI capabilities like computer vision – analysing visual data like images and video; speech recognition – transcribing spoken audio; and machine translation – automated translation between languages. But, compared to what's possible today, these advancements could be considered as revolutionary as my Panasonic dual-tape stereo was, if compared to the capabilities of the iTunes store.

While AI was going through "boom and bust" cycles, steady progress continued.

In the 2010s, we saw the rise of deep learning, which refers to neural networks with multiple layers that can learn highly complex relationships in data[11] – an approach that drew inspiration from neuroscience research. Although deep learning pre-dates the 2010s, around this time the field underwent significant advancements in its capabilities.[12] In contrast to earlier neural networks which were relatively shallow with few layers, later iterations of deep learning leveraged many stacked layers of computations. This layered architecture enabled major performance leaps, including the now-famous example of when an AI system called AlphaGo defeated the (human) world Go champion.[13] Go is an ancient Chinese strategy game that, despite simple rules, has a near infinite number of potential game configurations. To win the game, the human (or machine) requires strategic intuition and creative problem-solving. While many backed their money on human triumph, AlphaGo won the match[14] 4–1. AlphaGo achieved its breakthrough win by using a novel combination of algorithms and deep neural networks trained on thousands of human Go games (i.e. training data). This allowed it to look ahead at possible moves and countermoves, and intuitively evaluate board positions.

The landmark AlphaGo win signalled a major leap in AI advancement because AI could now surpass humans in highly strategic domains requiring intuition, not just raw computing power. Additionally, because Go was seen as a game requiring abstract reasoning skills, the win further signalled the potential of deep learning to deliver human-like cognition given enough training data. This level of skill was once thought unattainable for AI and led to enhanced enthusiasm for further advancing AI capabilities. Despite all the progress, AI capabilities remained far from matching human-level flexibility across all cognitive domains.

Looking at the historical trajectory reminds us how far AI capabilities have come. But it also highlights that realising the full aspirations of pioneers like Alan Turing and John McCarthy remains a quest requiring ongoing breakthroughs.

For many in academia, AI came onto the radar in late 2022, when OpenAI,[15] at the time a relatively unknown company, achieved notoriety in mainstream media after launching a product underpinned by a technology capable of disrupting multiple industry sectors.[16]

Even if you haven't used it, you're likely familiar with OpenAI's product, ChatGPT,[17] a conversation-style LLM that produces text (and more!) that ostensibly appears human-generated and does so at speeds that far exceed the capabilities of even the most talented touch typists.[18] Unprecedented public uptake of the technology ensued, making OpenAI's ChatGPT the fastest-growing application in history.[19] No less among student populations, who swiftly embraced the technology to complete their assignments.[20] It was primarily for this reason that from November 2022 onwards, ChatGPT's text-generation abilities sent the higher education sector into a period of paradigm-shifting revolution.

Or so I thought.

From my vantage point, I witnessed a surprising lag in response. Months passed before many academics began discussing AI, and when they did, many dismissed it as another passing trend. Given AI's growing influence,[21] I found the hesitation towards embracing an understanding of how it could be leveraged in academia rather strange, if not alarming – as I was increasingly concerned for the relevance of the higher education sector.

Tech enthusiasts and late-stage early adopters were exploring, and profiting from, AI's capabilities. Meanwhile, many in higher education focused their conversations on how students could potentially use this technology to bypass the integrity of traditional forms of academic assessment.[22] And while plagiarism conversations seem to largely sustain, in some circles these conversations soon expanded into discussions of how AI might impact the higher education sector more broadly.[23] As the capabilities of AI tools expanded, scholars increasingly began to realise that AI might be able to assist them in achieving many of their academic tasks.

Thus began a movement among some academics towards embracing AI technologies across multiple touchpoints of their academic work, including using AI chatbots to assist in writing academic papers. Those who openly admitted to doing so included several scholars who went as far as crediting ChatGPT as a co-author on their publications.[24] Although this attribution was quickly challenged despite some arguing for it meeting authorship criteria[25] – ChatGPT was deemed to lack the agency required for human authorship.[26] Regardless, these events brought scholarly use of AI into the spotlight, sparking curiosity, experimentation, and dialogue about AI's capabilities, not just for students, but for the academics responsible for governing future academic practice.

In my journey with AI, I've often found myself amazed at what these tools can accomplish with just a few clicks. My colleagues have shared similar experiences of awe. Yet, these moments of wonder tended to be tempered with feelings of uncertainty about the future of the higher education sector. These moments led me to ask, "Will AI continue to advance to the point where it replaces human skills and academic roles entirely?"

Reassuringly (although for how long remains anyone's guess), advancements in AI have not yet achieved the expansive general capabilities that were initially envisioned.[27] This is due to a range of factors, including the slow diffusion of AI's most impressive capabilities, the need for complementary innovations, and the challenges in integrating a broad range of cognitive capabilities into a coherent architecture.[28]

AI today excels as a specialist, demonstrating superhuman proficiency in narrow domains it has trained extensively in. For example, an AI can defeat the world's greatest chess grandmaster, translate languages in milliseconds, and create stunning works of digital art. But it cannot yet then shift to displaying the situational adaptability, well-rounded common sense, or interpersonal emotional intelligence that allows humans to thrive in the messy realities of everyday life. Current AI reasoning relies on patterns extracted from datasets, lacking the grounded understanding that comes from real-world experiences. This limitation can hinder AI's ability to respond flexibly to novel situations, and the general learning capabilities that humans develop during childhood, through interaction with the physical and social world, remain challenging to replicate in machines.

Despite these limitations, AI can be remarkably capable, or "scary smart" as AI expert Mo Gawdat describes in his book on AI's future impact.[29] The rapid pace of AI advancement makes it difficult to predict how long the current limitations will persist. For now, human cognition retains an edge in creatively connecting contextual information across domains, a task that narrow AI struggles with. Thus, the gap between artificial general intelligence and today's specialised AI systems remains significant.

Rather than viewing AI as a threat to human roles, I tend to see it as an opportunity to enhance our unique strengths – as an extension of our human capabilities. This idea comes from the Extended Mind Thesis, introduced by philosophers Andy Clark and David Chalmers, which posits that cognitive functions can extend beyond the biological brain to incorporate external tools and resources. Essentially, AI could be considered an external object that actively aids our thinking and guides our cognition, thus extending our cognitive architecture beyond the traditional boundaries of our minds.[30]

AI-enhanced academic roles

While artificial intelligence has made great strides, it cannot yet replicate the full range of scholarly tasks and social nuances involved in the multi-faceted nature of academic work.

Trust me, I've tried!

Within the bounds of its current abilities, AI remains sitting in the passenger seat,[31] even if it might be autonomously driving the car.

The array of responsibilities spanning teaching, research, collaboration, and university service appear secure from wholesale automation. An academic's role extends beyond processing information or generating publications. Our ability for original theorising, contextual synthesis of concepts, the ability to design rigorous studies aligned to ethical review board requirements, critically evaluating evidence, and communicating complex ideas (which is a long, but far from exhaustive list of hats we wear) all draw upon accumulated human training in scholarly methods and also reflect our disciplinary quirks.

Moreover, we mustn't underestimate the value of human elements like mentorship, debate, and interpersonal rapport which underpins scholarly work. Fingers crossed, students will continue to seek out the wisdom of their supervisors and extended academic community rather than solely relying on chatbots for advice. Thus, while AI promises to enhance certain academic tasks, the essence of scholarly work remains profoundly human.

While AI may not be capable of replicating human academics, it is reasonable to expect that academics who fail to keep pace with shifting work practices will fall behind.

Take, for example, two fellowship candidates where one is highly AI literate while the other dismisses AI tools as trendy gadgets. Putting aside other entries in their resumés, it seems clear which would be better placed to contribute to an institution that's operating in a period where AI is increasingly entering all aspects of university operations. Any scholar integrating AI for efficiencies like automated admin, data analysis, or writing assistance will likely be at a competitive advantage over less tech-savvy peers because AI affords knowledge workers the ability to complete tasks at greater speed and efficiency.[32] Though AI cannot wholly substitute academics, scholars who ignore developing capabilities may find themselves publishing less, winning fewer grants, and becoming outmoded in comparison to their AI-literate peers.

Amidst this environment, I encourage you to judiciously welcome AI as a collaborator while safeguarding the aspects of your academic role that are most important to you. By cultivating AI skills, academics ensure they write their future rather than becoming relics replaced by thinking machines or displaced by AI-augmented peers.[33]

Can AI write my thesis or academic paper?

Before providing some examples of how AI can potentially assist you in your academic work, let's address the elephant in the room: "Can artificial intelligence write your PhD thesis or academic paper from start to finish?"

In short, "Yes it can!"

AI systems are currently capable of generating long-form text on demand on virtually any topic.[34] Putting aside the question of whether the AI-generated text would be any good, there are many reasons why taking a hands-off approach and letting AI entirely write such important and complex documents is ill-advised, not to mention highly problematic.[35] To explore this issue, let's examine some motivations for why you might want to outsource your writing to AI, from the perspectives of a PhD candidate (Jane) and a tenured academic (Louise).

Jane's PhD candidature journey

As a fledgling PhD candidate, Jane faces immense pressure to produce written work. The lengthy thesis can feel like an insurmountable mountain to climb, and Jane spends long hours reading literature and taking notes but struggles to synthesise concepts and articulate her ideas. She watches as peers effortlessly produce page after page while she agonises over each paragraph.

The temptation arises to let an AI system quickly generate paragraphs or even entire chapters that she can then polish up and submit.

She's heard that's possible.

Why not give it a go?

Well, aside from a host of ethical quandaries associated with one-click text generation,[36] one of the key problems with Jane using AI merely as an automated writing tool is that doing so overlooks a core purpose of the PhD journey: the apprenticeship of becoming an independent researcher.

The doctoral process is as much about developing critical research skills as it is about producing the final dissertation, noting that the two are very much an interwoven process. Bypassing the analytical thinking needed to synthesise concepts, identify gaps, and then articulate ideas through the writing process (i.e. outsourcing that work to AI) cheats Jane out of an enriching scholarly experience.

Yes, the thesis document needs to be written, and many of the tasks involved in its creation *could* be outsourced to AI to accelerate (or replace) the process. However, the skills picked up along the learning journey towards producing the thesis are what will sustain and advance Jane's career long term.

If she gains an academic role post-PhD, it's the research and writing skills honed during her PhD candidature that will enable her to continue to grow, not the final thesis itself. In other words, while submitting the thesis document is her ticket to entry into the academy, once inside, nearly everyone holds that ticket. Jane's competitive advantage will be characterised by the skills she's acquired in the process. As such, rather than viewing AI as an automated author, a more strategic approach would be for Jane to use AI as a collaborative assistant; a tool with which to amplify her abilities.

Louise's tenured academic journey

Unlike Jane, Louise has already earned her PhD and achieved tenure as a professor at a prestigious university. She has a solid grasp of her field and extensive experience conducting original research and publishing academic papers. However, Louise feels immense pressure to continuously publish to maintain her position and progress in her career. The prospect of letting an AI system generate draft papers is enticing. Why should she waste time on the tedious process of writing literature reviews, or methods sections, when AI can quickly produce those components of her work?

Louise may be well-justified in rationalising that she already knows how to conduct rigorous research, however, she should be wary of fully outsourcing her writing to AI for several reasons. Firstly, writing remains a critical part of Louise's thought process and a way to clarify and deepen her ideas. By skipping the writing, she loses opportunities for scholarly insights. Secondly, academic writing requires making nuanced rhetorical choices to effectively convey complex concepts and arguments to readers. Advanced knowledge and critical thinking are needed to organise ideas logically, choose words judiciously, and adapt the tone of writing for different audiences. As yet, AI is hard-pressed to replicate Louise in her pursuit of those tasks. Thirdly, transparency and ethics demand that Louise take responsibility for the final published work bearing her name. While scholars may opt to turn to AI as a black box for churning out papers, Louise holds the scholarly process in high regard. Thus, while AI offers the potential for productivity gains, Louise is also mindful that she doesn't wish to outsource the core of her academic work.

Rather than using AI to generate fully written papers, a better approach may be for Louise to use AI as an assistive tool, used to collaborate on writing tasks, leaving her in control over the process, and removing any doubt that she is the unquestionable author of the papers she puts into the world.

In examining the perspectives of both Jane and Louise, we see good reasons to pull back from the idea of fully automating academic writing with AI tools. Beyond the ethical responsibility needed to produce substantive scholarly work, both Jane and Louise would cheat themselves of enriching scholarly experiences by treating AI as a shortcut to publication. However, the above examples also illustrate how AI could be strategically incorporated as a tool to enhance, not replace, human skills and writing. To explore how this might be achieved, let's leave current-day AI for a moment to travel back to 1984, where guidance can be found for how Jane and Louise might effectively build their AI skills and become AI-powered scholars.

A framework for developing AI literacy

One method for acquiring the skills needed to use AI effectively can be found in the "Miyagi Framework", comprising the following tenets:

- break down complex skills into fundamental tasks,
- develop muscle memory through deliberate practice, and
- apply and combine the basics to execute advanced techniques.

If you haven't come across the Miyagi Framework before in academic research, that's probably because it's more commonly known as a popular culture touchstone. Mr Miyagi, from whom the framework takes its name, is a protagonist in the 1980s' cult classic, *The Karate Kid*, a film about Miyagi and his young pupil, Daniel.

When Daniel faces challenges in his life, the sage Miyagi takes him under his wing to school him in the art of Karate.

Eager to commence his training, Daniel turns up to his first class, full of enthusiasm, only to find that Miyagi wishes Daniel to wash his fleet of vintage cars. To complete the chore, Daniel is instructed to use specific hand movements, delivered by the famous film quote "Wax on, wax off". Although frustrated to learn that his Karate aspirations are temporarily on hold, Daniel obliges Miyagi and engages in the task with the expectation that doing a good job should surely lead to the commencement of his official training.

When the next day arrives, Daniel's hopes of learning to become a Karate master are put on hold again as Miyagi assigns another chore to his pupil. Handing Daniel two sanding discs, Miyagi provides clear instructions for how the sanding should be conducted, "Right circle, left circle". To which Daniel replies, "Wouldn't it be easier going back and forth?" demonstrating his lack of awareness of Miyagi's stealth training methods.

Seemingly conned out of another day of Karate training, Daniel completes the task, leaves disgruntled, but returns with renewed hope that *finally* his training can begin. Yet, despite his hopes, disappointment ensues as Miyagi hands Daniel a paintbrush and tin and instructs him to spend his next day of training painting fences. When Daniel finally reaches the limits of his youthful patience, he erupts in protest, claiming he hasn't learned a thing.

If you're familiar with the movie, you'll also be familiar with Miyagi's formative pedagogical approach to fostering skill development. With each chore, unbeknownst to Daniel, Miyagi was helping Daniel build the muscle memory and reflexes required to tackle any Karate move thrown his way.

It's through the lens of the Miyagi Framework that I offer you a series of skill-development activities in this book. Each is designed to develop your muscle memory and AI reflexes. However, unlike the naive Daniel who laboured through his training without knowledge that each task was building towards mastery, you're invited to enter the journey fully aware that you have some car waxing, deck sanding, and fence painting to do before getting in the AI ring.

Before proceeding to the next chapter, take a moment to reflect on the concepts we've explored. The questions offered in the "Reflection and discussion" section below are designed to deepen your understanding and encourage critical thinking about the role of AI in academia. Consider discussing these with colleagues to gain diverse perspectives.

Reflection and discussion

The following questions are presented for personal reflection and can also be used to spark discussion of the topics covered in this chapter within a classroom setting.

1. Discuss the ethical implications of using AI in academic writing. How might this affect the integrity and originality of scholarly work?
2. Compare and contrast the potential benefits and risks of AI use for early career researchers (like Jane) versus established academics (like Louise).
3. How might the integration of AI tools in academia influence the development of critical thinking and research skills in students and early career researchers?
4. Discuss the concept of AI as an extension of human cognitive capabilities (as per the Extended Mind Thesis). How might this perspective change our approach to using AI in academic work?
5. What skills do you think will be most valuable for academics in an AI-augmented future? How can these skills be developed?

Activity

If you're working through this book with friends or in a classroom setting, I encourage you to engage with the activities provided at the end of each chapter.

Activity: AI in academia role-play

Objective: To explore the potential uses, benefits, and challenges of integrating AI into academic work from various perspectives.

Instructions:

1. Form small groups of 3–4 participants.
2. Assign roles within each group, for example:

- PhD candidate or early-career researcher
- Tenured professor
- University ethics committee member
- Academic journal editor

3. Scenario: Your university is developing guidelines for the use of AI in academic writing and research. Each group needs to create a proposal for these guidelines.
4. Role-play discussion (30 minutes):
   - Each participant should advocate from their assigned perspective.
   - Consider how AI might be integrated into different aspects of academic work (e.g. literature review, data analysis, writing, peer review).
   - Discuss potential benefits and risks.
   - Address how academic integrity could be maintained while benefiting from AI tools.
5. Develop guidelines (15 minutes):
   - Based on your discussion, create a short list of 5–7 guidelines for AI use in academic work.
6. Share and compare (15 minutes):
   - Each group presents their guidelines to the larger class.
   - Discuss similarities and differences between group proposals.
7. Reflection (10 minutes):
   - Individually, write a brief reflection on how this activity has influenced your perspective on AI in academia.
   - Consider how you might apply these insights, or adopt the developed guidelines, in your academic research or teaching roles.

Notes

1. A chatbot is an AI program designed to simulate conversation, primarily through text but also potentially through voice, images, or other modalities. In this chapter, we focus on text-based LLMs.
2. Riskin, J. (2003). The defecating duck, or, the ambiguous origins of artificial life. *Critical Inquiry*, *29*(4), 599–633. https://doi.org/10.1086/377722

3. Turing, A. (1950). I.—Computing machinery and intelligence. *Mind, LIX*(236), 433–460. https://doi.org/10.1093/mind/lix.236.433
4. McCarthy, J. M., Minsky, M. L., Rochester, N., & Shannon, C. E. (1955). *A Proposal for the Dartmouth Summer Research Project on Artificial Intelligence*. https://www-formal.stanford.edu/jmc/history/dartmouth/dartmouth.html
5. Copeland, B. J. (2023). Early AI in Britain: Turing et al. *IEEE Annals of the History of Computing, 45*(3), 19–31. https://doi.org/10.1109/mahc.2023.3300660
6. Anyoha, R. (2017, August 28). The history of artificial intelligence. *Harvard Graduate School of Arts and Sciences – Science in the News*. https://sitn.hms.harvard.edu/flash/2017/history-artificial-intelligence/
7. Crevier, D. (1993). *AI: The tumultuous history of the search for artificial intelligence*. Basic Books. https://www.researchgate.net/publication/233820788_AI_The_Tumultuous_History_of_the_Search_for_Artificial_Intelligence
8. Dreyfus, H. L. (1992). *What Computers Still Can't Do: A Critique of Artificial Reason*. MIT press.
9. Mitchell, M. (2021, April 26). *Why AI Is Harder Than We Think*. arXiv.org. https://arxiv.org/abs/2104.12871
10. Müller, B., Reinhardt, J., & Strickland, M. T. (2012). *Neural Networks: An Introduction*. Springer Science & Business Media.
11. LeCun, Y., Bengio, Y., & Hinton, G. E. (2015). Deep learning. *Nature, 521*(7553), 436–444. https://doi.org/10.1038/nature14539
12. Alzubaidi, L., Zhang, J., Humaidi, A. J., Al-Dujaili, A. Q., Duan, Y., Al-Shamma, O., Santamaría, J., Fadhel, M. A., Al-Amidie, M., & Farhan, L. (2021). Review of deep learning: Concepts, CNN architectures, challenges, applications, future directions. *Journal of Big Data, 8*(53), 1–74. https://doi.org/10.1186/s40537-021-00444-8
13. Silver, D., Schrittwieser, J., Simonyan, K., Antonoglou, I., Huang, A., Guez, A., Hubert, T., Baker, L. R., Lai, M., Bolton, A., Chen, Y., Lillicrap, T. P., Fan, H., Sifre, L., Van Den Driessche, G., Graepel, T., & Hassabis, D. (2017). Mastering the game of Go without human knowledge. *Nature, 550*(7676), 354–359. https://doi.org/10.1038/nature24270
14. Borowiec, S. (2017, November 29). AlphaGo seals 4-1 victory over Go grandmaster Lee Sedol. *The Guardian*. https://www.theguardian.com/technology/2016/mar/15/oogles-alphago-seals-4-1-victory-over-grandmaster-lee-sedol

15. https://openai.com
16. Agrawal, A. (2022, December 14). ChatGPT and how AI disrupts industries. *Harvard Business Review*. https://hbr.org/2022/12/chatgpt-and-how-ai-disrupts-industries
17. ChatGPT is an AI language model developed by OpenAI that can engage in human-like text conversations, answer questions, and assist with various tasks across a wide range of topics, available at https://openai.com/chatgpt/. While ChatGPT is used as the primary example in this book due to its widespread recognition, it's important to note that there are numerous other chatbots available. These include Anthropic's Claude and Google's Gemini, among others. Each of these AI models has its own unique features and capabilities. I encourage trialling multiple chatbots to find the one you like best, which suits your needs.
18. Chen, T. J. (2023). ChatGPT and other artificial intelligence applications speed up scientific writing. *Journal of the Chinese Medical Association, 86*(4), 351–353. https://doi.org/10.1097/jcma.0000000000000900
19. Gordon, C. (2023, February 2). ChatGPT is the fastest growing app in the history of web applications. *Forbes*. https://www.forbes.com/sites/cindygordon/2023/02/02/chatgpt-is-the-fastest-growing-ap-in-the-history-of-web-applications/?sh=32a03ec7678c
20. Eke, D. (2023). ChatGPT and the rise of generative AI: Threat to academic integrity? *Journal of Responsible Technology, 13,* 100060. https://doi.org/10.1016/j.jrt.2023.100060; Stokel-Walker, C. (2022). AI bot ChatGPT writes smart essays — should professors worry? *Nature*. https://doi.org/10.1038/d41586-022-04397-7
21 Walsh, T. (2023, November 30). A year of ChatGPT: 5 ways the AI marvel has changed the world. *The Conversation*. https://theconversation.com/a-year-of-chatgpt-5-ways-the-ai-marvel-has-changed-the-world-218805
22. Perkins, M. (2023). Academic integrity considerations of AI large language models in the post-pandemic era: ChatGPT and beyond. *Journal of University Teaching and Learning Practice, 20*(2), 1–26. https://doi.org/10.53761/1.20.02.07
23. Lund, B., Wang, T., Mannuru, N. R., Nie, B., Shimray, S. R., & Wang, Z. (2023). ChatGPT and a new academic reality: Artificial intelligence-written research papers and the ethics of the LLMs in scholarly publishing. *Journal of the Association for Information Science and Technology, 74*(5), 570–581. https://doi.org/10.1002/asi.24750

24. Stokel-Walker, C. (2023). ChatGPT listed as author on research papers: Many scientists disapprove. *Nature, 613*(7945), 620–621. https://doi.org/10.1038/d41586-023-00107-z
25. Polonsky, M. J., & Rotman, J. (2023). Should artificial intelligent (AI) agents be your co-author? Arguments in favour, informed by ChatGPT. *Social Science Research Network,* 1–14. https://doi.org/10.2139/ssrn.4349524
26. Thorp, H. H. (2023). ChatGPT is fun, but not an author. *Science, 379*(6630), 313. https://doi.org/10.1126/science.adg7879
27. Arel, I., & Livingston, S. (2009). Beyond the Turing test. *IEEE Computer, 42*(3), 90–91. https://doi.org/10.1109/mc.2009.67; Świechowski, M. (2022). Deep learning and artificial general intelligence: Still a long way to go. *arXiv (Cornell University),* 1–14. https://doi.org/10.48550/arxiv.2203.14963
28. Brynjolfsson, E., Rock, D., & Syverson, C. (2017). *Artificial Intelligence and the Modern Productivity Paradox: A Clash of Expectations and Statistics*. https://doi.org/10.3386/w24001
29. Gawdat, M. (2021). *Scary Smart: The Future of Artificial Intelligence and How You Can Save Our World*. Pan Macmillan.
30. Clark, A., & Chalmers, D. (1998). The extended mind. *Analysis, 58*(1), 7–19. http://www.jstor.org/stable/3328150
31. Chan, C. K. Y., & Tsi, L. H. Y. (2023). The AI revolution in education: Will AI replace or assist teachers in higher education? *arXiv (Cornell University),* 1–18. https://doi.org/10.48550/arxiv.2305.01185
32. Dell'Acqua, F., McFowland, E., Mollick, E., Lifshitz-Assaf, H., Kellogg, K. C., Rajendran, S., Krayer, L. J., Candelon, F., & Lakhani, K. R. (2023). Navigating the jagged technological frontier: Field experimental evidence of the effects of AI on knowledge worker productivity and quality. *Social Science Research Network,* 1–58. https://doi.org/10.2139/ssrn.457332; Noy, S., & Zhang, W. (2023). Experimental evidence on the productivity effects of generative artificial intelligence. *Social Science Research Network*. https://doi.org/10.2139/ssrn.4375283
33. Howard, J. (2019). Artificial intelligence: Implications for the future of work. *American Journal of Industrial Medicine, 62*(11), 917–926. https://doi.org/10.1002/ajim.23037; Taylor, A., Nelson, J., O'Donnell, S., Davies, E., & Hillary, J. (2022). The skills imperative 2035: What does the literature tell us about essential skills most needed for work? *Working Paper 1*. National Foundation for Educational Research.

34. Grimaldi, G., & Ehrler, B. (2023). AI et al.: Machines are about to change scientific publishing forever. *ACS Energy Letters*, *8*(1), 878–880. https://doi.org/10.1021/acsenergylett.2c02828; Kohda, Y., & Javed, A. (2023). To what extent can AI simplify academic paper writing? *AHFE International*, 1–10. https://doi.org/10.54941/ahfe1004194
35. Balel, Y. (2023). The role of artificial intelligence in academic paper writing and its potential as a co-author: Letter to the editor. *European Journal of Therapeutics*, *29*(4), 984–985. https://doi.org/10.58600/eurjther1691; Lee, J. Y. (2023). Can an artificial intelligence chatbot be the author of a scholarly article? *Journal of Educational Evaluation for Health Professions*, *20*, 6. https://doi.org/10.3352/jeehp.2023.20.6
36. Kooli, C. (2023). Chatbots in education and research: A critical examination of ethical implications and solutions. *Sustainability*, *15*(7), 5614. https://doi.org/10.3390/su15075614

3 Communicating effectively with AI

Introduction

Even among humans, miscommunication is a daily dance we all stumble through. A raised eyebrow, a subtle tone shift, or a cultural context can completely change the meaning of our words. Now, strip away all those non-verbal cues, remove shared life experiences, and try to convey your deepest academic insights using only your keyboard to guide your conversation.

In this chapter, we'll explore the fascinating – and sometimes frustrating – world of human-AI communication. We'll explore the pitfalls that can turn your carefully crafted instructions into digital lost-in-translation moments. Through an interactive activity, you'll experience firsthand how easily messages can go awry and discover strategies to bridge the gap between human intent and AI output. By the end of this chapter, you'll be better equipped with the skills to translate your academic goals into clear instructions that even the most literal-minded AI can understand.

Lost in translation

Let's begin with an activity called "Lost in Translation". It aims to demonstrate the challenges of conveying information accurately, even between humans, and sets the stage for understanding the complexities of communicating with AI.

DOI: 10.4324/9781032665276-3

Here's the premise: you'll draw a picture and then attempt to describe it verbally to a partner. Your partner's task is to recreate your drawing based solely on your spoken instructions. No peeking. No hand gestures. Just words!

Sounds straightforward, doesn't it?

You might be thinking, "How hard can it be to describe a simple drawing?"

Well, prepare to be surprised! This activity has a knack for exposing the gaps between what we think we're communicating and what others understand.

To get started, you'll need to find a willing partner. This could be a fellow academic, a friend, a family member, or a housemate. The beauty of this activity is that it works just as well with a colleague as it does with your nine-year-old niece.

Once you've recruited your partner and you're both ready to begin, here's a step-by-step guide to completing the activity:

1. Preparation: Each participant needs a blank sheet of paper and a pen or pencil.
2. Initial drawing: Set a timer for around 60 seconds. During this time, create a drawing on your paper. Be creative – use shapes, lines, or any design elements you wish. Keep your drawing hidden from your partner.
3. Role assignment: Decide who will be the "describer" and who will be the "drawer". The describer's task is to verbally guide the drawer in recreating the original drawing without showing it.
4. Description phase: The describer provides verbal instructions to the drawer. Focus on specific details such as shapes, sizes, positions, and angles. Use clear, precise language. The drawer should listen silently, only asking for clarification if absolutely necessary.
5. Drawing phase: As the describer speaks, the drawer attempts to recreate the original drawing based solely on the verbal instructions.
6. Comparison: Once complete, reveal both drawings and compare them side by side, and identify the similarities and differences between the original and the reproduction.
7. Analysis: Discuss the communication process. Identify what worked well and what led to misunderstandings as you moved towards replicating the drawing. Consider how the instructions could have been improved to achieve a more accurate reproduction.

8. Role reversal: Switch roles and repeat steps 4–7. The original drawer now becomes the describer.
9. Second comparison: Compare the new set of drawings, noting any improvements or persistent challenges in communication.
10. Reflection: Engage in a broader discussion about the experience. If in a group setting, share insights and observations with the larger class. Consider how this exercise relates to communication challenges in other contexts, including with AI systems.

Now that you've completed the activity, let's reflect on your experience:

1. Outcome analysis: How closely did the reproduced drawing match the original? Were there significant differences or surprising similarities?
2. Communication challenges: Did you encounter any unexpected difficulties in describing or interpreting the instructions? Were there moments where you felt your partner misunderstood your directions?
3. Specificity struggles: How did you fare when trying to convey precise details? Did you find yourself struggling to describe exact shapes, angles, or spatial relationships? What strategies did you use to overcome these challenges?
4. Language limitations: Did you feel constrained by vocabulary or struggle to find the right words? How did you adapt your language to make your instructions clearer?
5. Detail dilemma: How did you balance providing enough detail for accuracy without overwhelming your partner with information? Did you find yourself over-explaining or under-explaining certain elements?
6. Perspective problems: Did you encounter any issues related to perspective or point of view? How did you handle describing the overall layout versus specific elements of the drawing?

As explored below, these communication hurdles parallel the difficulties we face when interacting with AI systems.

Unpacking the activity

The "Lost in Translation" activity is a classic icebreaker that I use in my AI training workshops. And, despite the varied cultural backgrounds of participants, from chemists in Vienna to accountants in Auckland, key insights consistently emerge during the post-activity reflection and discussion. These universal takeaways (introduced below) highlight fundamental aspects of human communication, and, by extension, the challenges we can face when interacting with AI systems.

Text-based interactions omit verbal cues

A crucial insight from this activity is the significant role non-verbal cues play in our daily communications. Facial expressions, gestures, and other visual signals often convey as much meaning as our words. However, when interacting with AI through text prompts, we lose these familiar cues entirely.

This loss of non-verbal communication adds a unique challenge to human-AI interactions, with research showing that people tend to use shorter, less nuanced instructions when communicating with computer interfaces compared to human conversations.[1] We typically rely heavily on non-verbal cues like gestures, facial expressions, and body language to convey meaning.[2] Yet, when communicating with AI, our communication toolkit can become limited to words alone. As such, much like the "drawer" in our activity who relied solely on verbal instructions, when interacting with AI tools, we can find ourselves communicating without the benefit of body language or subtext interpretation. This necessitates a more direct, specific, and clear approach to our instructions if we wish to achieve our desired results.

Effectively communicating with AI requires a bit of a micro shift, wherein we break down our larger goals and complex ideas into logically sequenced, precise, and unambiguous instructions that AI can interpret and execute. This "translational thinking" forms the foundation of effective prompt writing, a skill we'll explore in depth in Chapter 6.

Better results are achieved when using unambiguous language

Another hurdle participants tend to encounter during the drawing activity is the ambiguity inherent in many commonly used words – similarly challenging when interacting with AI systems.[3]

Unlike humans, AI lacks the real-world experience needed to intuitively disambiguate words based on context (if that context is lacking). This limitation has linguistic roots – the complex evolutionary history of English incorporating diverse influences has led to many words taking on multiple meanings and nuances.[4] Additionally, for AI systems, language exists as raw computer code without intrinsic meaning. Thus, devoid of embodied human experience, current-day AI lacks our innate sense to infer intended meanings for ambiguous words. This creates a communication barrier when we provide ambiguous instructions to AI.[5] For example, asking an AI system to "Draw a ball" could yield results ranging from playground balls to crystal balls, depending on its interpretation. To reduce confusion, it's important to communicate unambiguously by using precise words and phrases that delineate meaning within the given context. Providing clarifying details and examples further constrains the semantic scope of our language. As such, rather than saying "Draw a ball", it might be better to use an instruction like, "Draw a tennis ball with a yellow fuzzy texture".

By consciously minimising the room for multiple interpretations, we enable smoother exchanges where our intentions align with AI-generated outcomes.

Smaller steps guide AI towards achieving larger goals

Reflect on your experience during the drawing activity. You likely guided your partner through a step-by-step process, beginning with a key element and gradually adding more detailed descriptions. Expecting your partner to accurately recreate the entire drawing from a single, all-encompassing instruction is rather unrealistic.

This insight directly translates to effective communication with AI systems. While AI models can be highly capable of handling complex tasks, if we were to provide only a single instruction (i.e. a zero-shot prompt), we are unlikely to be able to achieve overly complex tasks, or receive suboptimal outputs in response to our requests.

While zero-shot prompts can be effective for simple tasks, they often fall short for more complex objectives. Instead of trying to get the AI to do everything at once, breaking down your larger goal into smaller, incremental steps/instructions can lead to more accurate and useful outputs.

This approach, sometimes called chain of thought prompting, allows you to guide the AI more precisely through each stage of the task.

To implement this strategy, consider doing the following:

1. Start by clearly outlining your overarching objective.
2. Break this goal down into a series of smaller, manageable sub-tasks.
3. Craft specific instructions for each sub-task, ensuring they build upon each other logically.
4. Provide context or examples where necessary to clarify your expectations.

This approach not only improves the accuracy of AI-generated outputs but also gives you more control over the process, allowing for adjustments and refinements at each step.

Providing examples can help align outputs to inputs

A key observation from the drawing activity is the power of specific examples in enhancing understanding and accuracy. This insight is particularly relevant when communicating with AI systems.

Consider the difference between these two instructions:

1. "Draw a house".
2. "Draw a red brick house with a grey shingled roof, white picket fence, and smoke curling from the chimney".

The first instruction is rather vague and open to wide interpretation. It could result in anything from a suburban mansion to a child's playhouse. The second instruction, however, provides more detail that guides the drawer (or AI) towards a particular outcome.

When interacting with AI chatbots, providing examples can assist with, for example:

1. Establishing clear boundaries: Define the scope and style of the desired output, reducing the AI's tendency to generate irrelevant or off-topic content.

2. Setting concrete goals: Give the AI a clear target to aim for, improving the relevance and quality of its output.
3. Demonstrating desired formats or structures: Examples show the AI how you want information presented or should be organised.
4. Clarifying abstract concepts: Complex or nuanced ideas become more tangible when illustrated with concrete examples.
5. Reducing ambiguity: Specific examples can lessen the chances of misinterpretation or unintended outputs.

Remember, the quality of your examples can directly influence the quality of the AI's output, so aim to choose examples that closely align with your desired outcome. Furthermore, don't hesitate to refine or provide additional examples if the initial results aren't satisfactory.

Communicating perspective helps shape AI-generated outputs

The drawing activity also reveals some insight into how we see the world: our perspective. When delivering this activity in a classroom, if you request participants to draw their journey to work that day, they typically adopt a first-person viewpoint, depicting landmarks as they would see them from inside a vehicle. However, when describing this scene to their partner, the replicated drawing rarely takes the same perspective. The "drawer" interprets the instructions and tries to reproduce the image, but from *their* perspective – looking at the scene, rather than from within it, or by providing a bird's-eye view.

When engaging with an AI tool, you might consider specifying a perspective you want it to adopt (explored further in Chapter 4). This applies to various aspects of content generation, including:

1. Narrative voice: Clearly state whether you want content in first-person, second-person, or third-person perspective.
2. Temporal perspective: Specify if you need a historical overview, current analysis, or future projection.
3. Cultural lens: Indicate if you need a particular cultural viewpoint or a multicultural approach.

4. Theoretical framework: Specify the academic or philosophical stance you want the AI to adopt (e.g., feminist theory, post-colonial perspective, or behaviourist approach).
5. Stakeholder viewpoint: In policy or business contexts, you might need to specify which stakeholder's perspective should be prioritised.

By defining the perspective, you guide the AI to generate content that hopefully aligns more closely with your intentions and needs.

However, despite how clear we may be, it's important to note the issue of bias in AI systems.

AI models are trained on vast datasets of human-generated content, which inevitably contain societal biases. When you specify a perspective, you may inadvertently trigger or amplify these biases. For example, if you ask an AI to write from a "traditional business leadership perspective", it might generate content that reflects gender biases prevalent in traditional business literature.[6] Similarly, requesting a "historical perspective" on a topic might result in a Eurocentric view if the AI's training data is skewed towards Western historical accounts. We'll explore this further in Chapter 7. For now, it's just important to know that these biases exist.

To mitigate biases, aim to:

1. Be aware of potential biases in your chosen perspective.
2. Explicitly request diverse viewpoints or counterarguments.
3. Critically evaluate the AI's output for unintended biases.
4. Consider using multiple, contrasting perspectives to get a more balanced view.

Using natural language aids human-AI communication

In the drawing activity, participants instinctively use conversational language to guide their partners. This natural, fluid communication style comes effortlessly in human-to-human interactions. However, when using AI tools, many people initially resort to terse, keyword-based prompts reminiscent of how many of us are used to performing a Google search. This shift in communication style can significantly limit the effectiveness of AI interactions.

Modern AI systems, particularly large language models (LLMs), are designed to understand and respond to natural, conversational language. These models are trained on vast corpora of human-written text, including books, articles, and online discussions, which enables them to grasp nuances, context, and intent in natural language.[7]

The benefits of using natural language with AI systems are numerous:

1. Improved understanding: AI models can better interpret your intent when you provide context and details in a conversational manner.
2. More nuanced responses: Natural language prompts allow the AI to pick up on subtleties and respond with more contextually appropriate information.
3. Reduced cognitive load: You don't need to learn a special 'AI language' or syntax; you can interact as you would with a human colleague.

It's worth noting that while AI systems excel at processing natural language, they don't truly "understand' in the way humans do. They generate responses based on patterns in their training data. This means they can sometimes produce fluent, plausible-sounding text that is factually incorrect or nonsensical. These are known as "hallucinations" and we'll explore this issue in the chapters ahead.

Providing context enhances the relevancy of generated content

In my AI workshops, I always begin the drawing activity by explaining its broader context and objectives – aiming to create a framework of understanding for what we'll be doing. By providing this information, participants understand the purpose of the activity, their roles within it, and what they need to achieve.

Context-setting can be equally important when interacting with AI systems. Unlike humans, who can draw upon shared cultural knowledge or intuitive understanding, AI models heavily rely on the information we provide them to understand what they should do for us.

By providing context, you're effectively "priming" the AI model. This allows the model to filter its vast knowledge base and focus on generating content that's most relevant to your specific needs. It's akin to giving a human collaborator a detailed brief before starting a project.

Moreover, context-setting can help mitigate some of the inherent limitations of AI models:

- It reduces the likelihood of the AI generating irrelevant or off-topic content.
- It helps maintain consistency across multiple interactions or generated outputs.
- It can guide the AI towards using appropriate terminology or jargon for your field.
- It allows you to indirectly influence the ethical stance or perspective of the generated content.

Remember, the quality of the context you provide directly influences the quality of the AI's output. Be as clear and specific as possible, but also be prepared to refine your context-setting approach through trial and error.

Building a shared history enhances long-term communication

Lastly, when participants switch roles between describer and drawer, communication typically improves. This improvement stems from the shared experience and mutual understanding developed during the first round, creating a foundation of common reference points and expectations.

This concept of building a shared history is crucial in enhancing long-term communication, both in human interactions and when working with AI systems.

In human communication, this shared history forms naturally through repeated interactions, creating a rich context that allows for more nuanced and efficient communication over time.

In AI interactions, this shared history is paralleled by what's known as a 'context window'. A context window represents the AI's capacity to retain and reference information from earlier in the conversation. However, unlike human memory, an AI's context window is typically limited, and, depending on the AI tool you're using, may be contained to a single chat session. The exact size of this context window will vary depending on the specific AI model you're interacting with.

Key takeaways

The key takeaways from the 'Lost in Translation' activity can be broadly summarised with the following key points:

- When communicating with AI through text prompts be unambiguous.
- Use natural language/be conversational.
- Provide contextual framing.
- Offer representative examples.
- Break down larger instructions into single-focused tasks.
- Specify perspective.
- Build a shared history.

With practice, you'll learn to convey your intents clearly and minimise the chances of getting lost in translation.

Reflection and discussion

Before progressing to the next chapter, I encourage you to pause and reflect on the following questions. If you're working through this book with others, these questions can serve as a starting point for discussion:

1. Think about a time you've had a communication breakdown with someone, where your message was unclear or misunderstood. What factors contributed to the ineffective communication? How might those same challenges apply when communicating with AI solely through text (or voice) prompts?

2. This chapter discussed strategies like using unambiguous language, providing context, and giving examples when communicating with AI. Based on your learnings, try writing instructions for an AI assistant. Then, critically evaluate the instruction, comparing it to how you might ask a human to complete the same task. Consider ways you could rewrite your instruction to enhance its natural language tone.
3. This chapter discusses translating broad goals into specific AI instructions. Practice this translation process for a sample scenario, like breaking down the tasks involved in brainstorming ideas for a literature review. Try reducing each task to a single-focused action and sequence them in a logical order.

Notes

1. Hill, J., Ford, W. R., & Farreras, I. G. (2015). Real conversations with artificial intelligence: A comparison between human–human online conversations and human–chatbot conversations. *Computers in Human Behavior, 49*, 245–250. https://doi.org/10.1016/j.chb.2015.02.026
2. Jording, M., Hartz, A., Bente, G., Schulte-Rüther, M., & Vogeley, K. (2018). The "social gaze space": A taxonomy for gaze-based communication in triadic interactions. *Frontiers in Psychology, 9*, 1–8. https://doi.org/10.3389/fpsyg.2018.00226
3. Glassman, E L. (2023, September 5). Designing interfaces for human-computer communication: An on-going collection of considerations. *arXiv (Cornell University)*, 1–5. https://doi.org/10.48550/arxiv.2309.02257
4. Anderson, R. C. (1990). Inferences about word meanings. In *Psychology of Learning and Motivation* (pp. 1–16). https://doi.org/10.1016/s0079-7421(08)60245-5; Heylighen, F., & Dewaele, J. M. (2002). Variation in the contextuality of language: An empirical measure. *Foundations of Science, 7*, 293–340.
5. Dias, S. M., & Vieira, N. G. (2015). Concept lattices reduction: Definition, analysis and classification. *Expert Systems with Applications, 42*(20), 7084–7097. https://doi.org/10.1016/j.eswa.2015.04.044

6. Newstead, T., Eager, B., & Wilson, S. (2023). How AI can perpetuate – Or help mitigate – Gender bias in leadership. *Organizational Dynamics, 52*(4), 100998. https://doi.org/10.1016/j.orgdyn.2023.100998
7. Chatterjee, J., & Dethlefs, N. (2023). This new conversational AI model can be your friend, philosopher, and guide ... and even your worst enemy. *Patterns, 4*(1), 100676. https://doi.org/10.1016/j.patter.2022.100676

4 Designing your AI research assistant

Introduction

Imagine having unlimited research funds to hire your dream assistant. They're well-versed in many knowledge domains, enthusiastic, and available 24/7. Sounds perfect, right? But there's a catch – this assistant has no idea how you want them to work, which academic norms to follow, or which of their many skills to apply to your tasks.

If your new hire was human, you'd probably have written a position description before hiring them, and on their first day of work, you'd provide detailed instructions for how they should perform. Unfortunately, when we "hire" a chatbot (i.e. collaboratively use AI tools to help us get our tasks done), these same steps can easily get overlooked. This is why some people walk away from AI technologies, disillusioned by a chatbot's output. Yet others become lifelong champions of the technology.

The difference? Learning to craft the AI into your dream assistant and clearly communicating what you'd like it to do. In other words, assigning it a persona, and learning how to write effective instructional commands to let it know what it should do for you while it's acting in that role. If that all sounds a bit strange, don't worry – and please stick with me – it will hopefully be clearer by the end of the chapter!

Before we get into specifics, let's consider the scenario of approaching a stranger on the street and asking them to perform a task for you. Odd as it may sound, this situation can closely resemble your first interaction

DOI: 10.4324/9781032665276-4

with an AI chatbot. Both start with a blank slate – no context, no shared understanding, just potential waiting to be unlocked.

The helpful stranger scenario

Picture this: you're strolling down a busy city street when you spot a friendly-looking stranger. In a rush, you hand them a page of complex academic text and make an unusual request: "Could you please rephrase this text using simpler language?"

"Sure!" the stranger replies with a smile.

They quickly scan the dense text, jot down some notes, and hand back a rewritten version, patiently awaiting your feedback.

You review their work with hopeful expectations, but... oh dear. Your heart sinks a bit as you read. While the text is indeed simpler now, the revised wording seems to miss the original's nuanced meaning. What's more, it's not quite suitable for your intended audience.

This isn't what you wanted at all!

Perplexed by your apparent disappointment, the stranger apologises for missing the mark.

"I'm sorry", they say, looking a bit crestfallen.

> I thought I understood your request, but I seem to have missed your intent. Without knowing the broader context or your specific needs, I just wrote what I thought was the most likely option. What perspective or lens should I have applied in rephrasing this?

And you know what? The stranger has a point.

Without providing clarifying parameters, how could they possibly interpret your request correctly? For all they knew, you might have wanted a version suitable for children, or for a blog post. The possibilities were endless, and they just went with what they considered the most likely path to follow.

In this scenario, the failure wasn't necessarily in the stranger's response, but in the lack of detail provided to guide their response.

It's a bit like asking someone to cook you a meal without specifying any dietary requirements or preferences – you might end up with a perfectly good dish that's completely unsuitable for you.

When you approached the stranger and asked them to rephrase the text, they likely tackled the task based on their lifetime of knowledge and experience. Their approach would have been shaped by years of reading, writing, and language exposure, allowing them to analyse the content and formulate it in what they believed to be an understandable way. In essence, the stranger provided you with what they predicted to be the most likely response you desired.

This example is analogous to how AI tools may operate, should you ask them to rephrase text for you. The tools simply provide you with what they predict to be the most likely answer to your question or instructional command. Let's explore this further below.

Prediction machines

While both humans and chatbots generate text based on past exposure to language patterns, they differ in that humans possess genuine understanding, consciousness, and the ability to reason abstractly, whereas chatbots generate text based on statistical patterns without true comprehension.

The ability of AI to generate text is underpinned by prediction[1] – assessing statistical patterns obtained from analysing vast datasets. The data they are trained on comes from incredibly large bodies of text, books, websites, and more. AI models discern subtleties about how language flows based on this data.[2] For example, learning that, in English, "friendly" often precedes terms like "greeting", "smile", or "helpful", much more commonly than the word "banana".

By way of illustration, consider this example of how the training process allows large language models (LLMs) to identify statistical patterns and relationships between words.

Imagine that an LLM was trained on a simple dataset containing just the following two sentences:

- The quick brown fox jumped over the lazy dog.
- The slow yellow cat sat on the busy street.

Even from just these two examples, the model can start detecting some basic patterns, like:

- "The" frequently precedes descriptor words like colours and speeds.
- Animated verbs like "jumped" and "sat" often follow the descriptor words.
- Prepositions like "over" and "on" transition to locations after the verbs.

Given the above training data, if the LLM was provided with the string of words "The speedy white rabbit", it might be more likely to follow it with words like "hopped through" and "the forest" based on the patterns it recognised, even though those exact sentences might not be in its training data.

This process involves internalising probabilities about which word will follow the next, allowing AI models to rate potential next words and phrases for the likelihood of sensibly responding to your entered prompts. The process is based on mathematics that's far beyond the scope of this book. All you really need to know as a nascent AI user is that as text inputs grow sentence by sentence, models combine optimal word guesses iteratively.

Before long, through cascading probabilistic predictions, coherent prose gets generated autonomously. Yet, it's important to remember that while these outputs may sound convincingly conversational (i.e. human generated), the AI holds no true grasp of the meaning behind the words.[3] It simply predicts the most statistically reasonable phrase continuations based on prior language patterns learned from training data at a massive scale.

This probabilistic approach to language generation is what allows AI models to produce coherent and contextually appropriate responses to a wide range of prompts. However, it's crucial to understand that this is fundamentally different from human language production, which is grounded in genuine understanding, intent, and the ability to reason about the world. While AI can mimic these abilities to a remarkable degree, it remains, at its core, a sophisticated pattern recognition and prediction system.

Designing your ideal research assistant

One effective way to guide AI tools, particularly AI chatbots, in providing you with useful content is to assign them a specific role. These roles act as filters through which the AI calculates the most statistically probable result you're seeking, thus helping it focus its lens and heighten its success in aligning the content it subsequently generates to meet your needs. The more specific and detailed you are in guiding an AI chatbot to understand the role you want it to assume, the less likely you are to experience disappointment due to misalignment or misunderstanding. This specificity helps bridge the gap between your expectations and the AI's output, reducing the chances of getting "lost in translation", as we explored in the previous chapter.

In the context of academic research, crafting detailed role descriptions can transform AI chatbots into your ideal research assistants. By assigning a role, you're essentially providing the AI with a framework within which to operate, much like you would brief a human research assistant on their responsibilities and expectations when they turn up for their first day of work.

When you assign a role, you are essentially asking the chatbot to "act" a certain part, akin to a director assigning a role to an actor. This role-playing approach gives the chatbot clear direction on how to align its generated text with your expectations.

There are endless characteristics you could specify when assigning a role, but rather than be overwhelmed with options, consider using the following equation for initial guidance[4]:

Role = Expertise + Background + Experience + Voice (optional)
+ Quirks (optional)

Let's explore each of these components in more detail:

1. Expertise: This defines the specialised knowledge or skills your AI assistant should possess. For instance, you might specify "A published author skilled in academic writing", "Qualitative research methods guru", or "Thematic analysis expert".
2. Background: This outlines the disciplinary context your AI assistant should be familiar with. Examples include "Economics PhD supervisor", "Practice-based nursing academic", or "Scholarly editor".
3. Experience: This determines the level of seniority or depth of knowledge your AI assistant should have. You might specify "A senior research assistant", "A subject matter expert in accounting", or "A professor who has dedicated their life to the field of developmental psychology".

4. Voice: This optional characteristic defines how your AI assistant should communicate. Options might include "Academic tone", "Plain English", or "Conversational".
5. Quirks: Another optional characteristic, this allows you to assign specific behavioural traits to your AI assistant. For example, you might want it to be "Funny", "Inspirational", or to "Play devil's advocate".

By carefully combining these role dimensions, you can create a unique persona tailored to your specific research needs.

The key is to be as specific and detailed as possible when defining the characteristics you want embodied in the AI's responses.

For example, consider the difference between these two role assignments:

1. "Act in the role of a research assistant".
2. "Act in the role of a senior research assistant with expertise in qualitative methodologies, particularly phenomenology. You have a background in sociology and five years of experience working on projects related to urban gentrification. Communicate in an academic tone but be prepared to explain complex concepts in simpler terms if asked".

The second prompt provides a much richer context for the AI to work within, likely resulting in more targeted and useful responses.

Remember, while this approach can significantly enhance the AI's performance, it doesn't alter the fundamental nature of how the AI operates. It is still using its training data and probabilistic models to generate responses, but now it's doing so through the lens of the assigned role, which helps to narrow and focus its outputs.

Below are some suggestions for different ways you could express each dimension of the role assignment equation: Role = Expertise + Background + Experience + Voice (optional) + Quirks (optional)

Expertise examples:

- Skilled academic writing scholar
- Literature review specialist

- Methodology advisor
- Gender theory expert
- Ethics advisor

Background examples:

- Entrepreneurship
- Marketing psychology
- Political sociology
- Applied anthropology
- Higher education pedagogy

Experience examples:

- Tenured professor
- Seasoned theorist
- Qualitative guru
- Experienced editor
- Knowledgeable librarian

Voice examples:

- Conversational
- Professional
- Academic
- Plain language
- Friendly

Quirks examples:

- Nerdy sense of humour
- Motivational and inspiring
- Prone to tangents

- Quotes poets and philosophers
- Uses positivity and encouragement

Combining variables from the above suggestions lets us create detailed role descriptions with which we can guide AI tools towards becoming our dream research assistants. Here are some examples:

- "Assume the identity of a qualitative expert with a specialisation in skilled academic writing. Adopt an academic and analytical voice to dissect complex qualitative data. As a respected supervisor and published author, use your wise perspective to mentor others in crafting compelling academic narratives, and don't hesitate to quote poets and philosophers to illustrate your points".
- "Embody the role of mixed methods extraordinaire who is also a literature review specialist. Take on a professional and objective voice to guide users through the intricacies of combining qualitative and quantitative data in academic writing. As someone who gets existential at times, weave in philosophical musings about the nature of research and evidence".
- "Take on the persona of an ethics advisor with a deep understanding of qualitative data analysis. Use a compassionate and encouraging voice to navigate the ethical dilemmas that can arise in qualitative research, particularly in sensitive areas like medical ethics or social policy. Infuse your dialogue with historical examples to provide context and depth".
- "Act in the role of a seasoned theorist and qualitative guru with a background in applied anthropology. Speak with a conversational yet academic tone, making complex qualitative theories accessible to a wider audience. As a knowledgeable librarian and skilled academic writer and scholar, sprinkle your conversations with nerdy humour and funny analogies to keep the discourse engaging".
- "Act in the role of an analytical mastermind with expertise in qualitative data visualisation and a background in higher education. Communicate with a technical and professional voice, translating qualitative insights into compelling narratives. As someone who loves to use funny analogies and knows random science trivia, make your explanations as informative as they are entertaining".

In addition to using the above examples, you might wish to save the role descriptions you create in a document, so they are easily accessed when, at a later date, you wish to perform another task for which that role would be ideal. You might also try adjusting the parameters within the role description, and then observing how even small tweaks can influence AI chatbot outputs.

With practice, you'll be able to manifest your ideal AI assistant for any given research context.

Ethical considerations

The practice of assigning personas to AI systems raises ethical concerns around identity and representation. Asking your AI chatbot to take on the role of "real" people may be problematic, depending on your intended use for the AI-generated outputs.

The personas assigned to AI can have real-world impacts, such as if controversial views are espoused without the original thinker's permission. Some popular examples include Australian music artist Nick Cave's identity being appropriated to generate song lyrics, much to his chagrin.[5] And AI being used to maliciously impersonate celebrities for scam-related criminal activities.[6]

When an AI adopts the identity of a real person without their consent, it can infringe on ethical boundaries, intellectual property rights, and individual autonomy. Generating output that seems to legitimately come from someone's perspective when it does not can enable the spread of misinformation, damage reputations, and undermine public trust.

When assigning AI personas based on real-life academics, practitioners, or public figures, you might consider the following:

- Do you have permission to co-opt their identity for use with AI? If not, is their representation accurate and respectful?
- Will persona responses be contextually appropriate and vetted for integrity? What controls are in place?
- Does the persona align with the individual's ethics and code of conduct?
- Could unauthorised use negatively impact the person's reputation or intellectual property?

Rather than appropriating real identities without consent, I suggest a safer approach of creating fictional personas comprising an amalgamation of real-world traits.

Lastly, when assigning personas, it's also important to remember that AI has no innate identity. Its "personhood" exists only insofar as humans project characteristics onto it through prompts and conditioning; AI systems like chatbots have no intrinsic experiences, beliefs, desires, or intentions. Chatbot persona's act as an illusion of personhood and help guide content creation.

Despite their machine nature, people often anthropomorphise AI. I'm guilty of this myself, and as you might have noticed throughout this book, I frequently slip into anthropomorphised references to AI. This is partly to provide you with a smoother reading experience, but also because I probably spend more time chatting with AI chatbots than humans, making them feel eerily human-like. Rest assured, I'm well aware they're not actually human.

A famous example of someone overestimating machine capabilities is Google engineer Blake Lemoine, who believed Google's LaMDA chatbot displayed signs of sentience after interacting with it.[7] Another example, albeit from fiction, is the movie "Her", where the protagonist falls in love with his AI assistant, Samantha.[8] However, romantic attachments to AI aren't limited to Hollywood. Replika, an AI chatbot app, allows users to create virtual partners.[9] Yes, you read that correctly: you can now date an AI. When the company issued an update to dial down the "romance" settings, some users reported feeling their companions had been lobotomised, leaving them extremely distressed. This event was dubbed the "Valentine's Day Massacre" – a term that speaks volumes about the emotional connections users can form with AI bots.

While it's easy to fall in love with the level of assistance AI can provide, it's probably a good idea to interact with AI tools in a way that's firmly grounded in reality. They are, at their core, sophisticated prediction machines – incredibly helpful, but not sentient beings.

Activity

After reading through this chapter, you're probably itching to test out your new persona-writing skills. Here's an activity to get started with:

Designing your dream research assistant

Try crafting a persona for your perfect research assistant by following the steps below.

1. First, write down descriptors for this fantasy assistant. What is their academic background? What about their tone of voice, expertise, quirks, or perspective do you want to include? Consider how those descriptors might influence the way an LLM responds to your requests for assistance.
2. Next, scope characteristics for your AI research assistant. Refer to the notes you jotted down earlier about your ideal assistant. Define their academic background, tone of voice, perspective, expertise, etc. Get creative!
3. Draft a "Act in the role of…" prompt, using natural language in the form of a sentence, or short paragraph. Use the example role prompts from this chapter, or the one below, to help draft your prompt.

   For example: "Act in the role of a knowledgeable mentor providing research advice to a new graduate student. Use simple, straightforward language and offer practical tips based on years of experience as an approachable and supportive mentor".

With practice, you can develop a repertoire of personas tailored to different contexts and conversational goals. The ability to essentially manifest your perfect research assistant on demand will take your AI collaboration to the next level.

Reflection and discussion

Use the following questions as a starting block to stimulate thinking and spark discussion:

1. How might assigning a persona to an AI chatbot impact the relevance and usefulness of its responses?
2. Think of a research task or project. If you had endless funds and the ability to transcend time, who would you hire to help you

complete the project? Describe their background, expertise, tone of voice, etc. Consider combining characteristics across multiple ideal hires to invent your dream fictional hire.

3. Try writing 2–3 sample "Act in the role of..." prompts for different research scenarios, such as literature reviews, data analysis, and academic writing. How might you word each persona?
4. What challenges might arise when using a single persona across multiple research tasks?

Notes

1. Agrawal, A., Gans, J., & Goldfarb, A. (2023, June 12). How large language models reflect human judgment. *Harvard Business Review*. https://hbr.org/2023/06/how-large-language-models-reflect-human-judgment; Mirchandani, S., Xia, F., Florence, P., Ichter, B., Driess, D., Arenas, M. G., Rao, K., Sadigh, D., & Zeng, A. (2023). Large language models as general pattern machines. *arXiv (Cornell University)*. https://doi.org/10.48550/arxiv.2307.04721
2. Johri, S. (2023, June 8). The making of ChatGPT: From data to dialogue. *Science in the News*. https://sitn.hms.harvard.edu/flash/2023/the-making-of-chatgpt-from-data-to-dialogue/
3. Mitchell, M. (2021). Why AI is harder than we think. *arXiv (Cornell University)*, 1–12. https://doi.org/10.48550/arxiv.2104.12871
4. Eager, B., & Brunton, R. (2023). Prompting higher education towards AI-augmented teaching and learning practice. Journal of University Teaching and Learning Practice, 20(5), 1–21. https://doi.org/10.53761/1.20.5.02
5. Savage, B. M. (2023, January 17). Nick Cave says ChatGPT's AI attempt to write Nick Cave lyrics "sucks". *BBC News*. https://www.bbc.com/news/entertainment-arts-64302944
6. Hsu, T., & Lu, Y. (2024, January 26). No, that's not Taylor Swift peddling le Creuset cookware. *The New York Times*. https://www.nytimes.com/2024/01/09/technology/taylor-swift-le-creuset-ai-deepfake.html

7. Tiku, N. (2023, May 23). The Google engineer who thinks the company's AI has come to life. *Washington Post*. https://www.washingtonpost.com/technology/2022/06/11/google-ai-lamda-blake-lemoine/
8. Ntelia, R. E. (2024). Love is in the AI of the Beholder Artificial Intelligence and characters of love. *E-REA, 21.2*. https://doi.org/10.4000/11wa6
9. Purtill, J. (2023, February 28). Replika users fell in love with their AI chatbot companions. Then they lost them. *ABC News*. https://www.abc.net.au/news/science/2023-03-01/replika-users-fell-in-love-with-their-ai-chatbot-companion/102028196

A brief history of conversational AI

Introduction

From science fiction to everyday reality, the journey of conversational AI has been nothing short of remarkable. As we find ourselves at a moment in time where chatting with an AI feels as natural as texting a friend, it's easy to forget the decades of innovation and perseverance that brought us here. Reflecting on this timeline, this chapter traces the evolution of conversational AI, offering both a historical perspective and an appreciation for the technology that many of us now take for granted.

Understanding the history of AI is crucial for several reasons. Importantly, it provides essential context for comprehending the capabilities and limitations of modern AI systems. By exploring key milestones and breakthroughs, we can better appreciate the rapid advancements of recent years and more accurately anticipate future developments. This foresight allows us to prepare for the integration of AI into our future academic workflows. Additionally, gaining insight into AI from a historical perspective lets us not only understand the technical progress that's occurred in the field of AI but also the persistent challenges and considerations that have accompanied its development. We'll be focusing on the fundamental developments and principles underlying modern AI chatbots, setting the stage for a deeper understanding of how to effectively interact with and leverage these powerful tools in academic contexts in future chapters.

Let's begin the journey by first clarifying what's meant by the term "conversational AI".

DOI: 10.4324/9781032665276-5

What is conversational AI?

Conversational-style AI, often referred to as "conversational AI" or "chatbots", represents a category of artificial intelligence designed to interact with humans through natural language.

These systems are built to understand, process, and generate human-like text or speech, enabling them to engage in dialogue that mimics human conversation.

Unlike traditional computer interfaces that require specific commands or clicks, conversational AI allows users to communicate as they would with another person, using everyday language to ask questions, request information, or complete tasks. At its core, conversational AI strives to bridge the gap between human communication and computer processing, creating a more seamless and user-friendly interface for human-machine interaction.

While we may take the "chatty" capabilities of modern AI for granted, the journey to achieve this level of natural interaction has been long and complex, encompassing decades of research, innovation, and technological breakthroughs that contributed to creating the experiences we enjoy with AI today.

To get an idea of how far things have advanced, I invite you to imagine attempting to communicate with a computer in the 1960s. The experience would likely resemble an interaction with a particularly uncooperative vending machine – full of pre-programmed responses and devoid of genuine understanding. Now, fast forward to our present day, where we find ourselves engaging with AI chatbots like ChatGPT, capable of discussing topics ranging from quantum physics or indulging us in writing quirky poems. The progress is nothing short of astonishing.

While modern-day chatbots such as ChatGPT showcase remarkably advanced natural language capabilities (for the latest ChatGPT updates, visit https://openai.com/research), the fundamental technique of text-based prompting actually traces back several decades; the AI models we interact with today are built upon the groundwork laid by early pioneers in the field – researchers and technologists who envisioned machines capable of engaging in meaningful conversation with humans.

Interestingly, despite the dramatic transformation of AI itself (imagine a caterpillar metamorphosing into a butterfly, but with more silicon involved), the basic prompting approach – the two-way communication between humans and machines – remains surprisingly recognisable. At least from a user's perspective. It's as if we've been engaged in the same game of conversational tennis for decades, and this continuity in approach persists despite the vast improvements in AI's capabilities and sophistication.

In the early stages of development, chatbots were about as flexible as a brick wall, relying on simple scripted responses. You would input a query, and they would promptly generate a pre-programmed reply with mechanical efficiency. Now, however, modern natural language processing allows for flexible, contextual conversations that can occasionally leave one pondering whether they're engaging with a machine or a particularly eloquent human interlocutor.

In essence, conversational AI can be thought of like the Swiss Army knife of the digital world – it's a multi-faceted tool designed to engage in meaningful and natural dialogues with humans.

But what makes these conversational AI systems tick? Let's break it down:

- Natural language processing: This is the AI's ability to "understand" our text or spoken words. It's like giving the AI a universal translator for human communication.
- Contextual awareness: This allows the AI to follow the flow of a conversation, much like how you keep track of what your friend is talking about over coffee (assuming you're not staring at your phone!).
- Generative skills: This is the AI's ability to craft relevant, personalised, and coherent responses. It's not just parroting information but synthesising it into something new and appropriate.
- Interactive interfaces: These are the digital platforms where you engage with the AI, typically through a chat window or text box on a screen. They're designed to mimic the back-and-forth nature of human conversation, allowing you to type your messages and receive the AI's responses in real-time. The goal is to make the interaction feel as natural and intuitive as conversing with a friend, despite the fact that you're communicating with a machine.

Remember how we touched on the idea of AI prediction machines in the last chapter? Conversational AI uses this ability to sift through massive amounts of human dialogue data, learning patterns, and nuances. It's like the AI is eavesdropping on millions of conversations to learn how we communicate. This statistical learning is what allows the AI to handle nuanced language, adapt to context, and even improve its conversational skills over time.

While early conversational AIs were text-only (kind of like having a pen pal), we've now entered the era of multi-modal AI.[1] This means that AI can now interact through various modes, not just text, including voice, images, and video.

In this book, though, we'll be focusing on text-based conversations. Why? Because mastering text interactions with AI chatbots is like learning to walk before you run – it's a fundamental skill that will serve you well in your journey to becoming an AI-savvy scholar.

A timeline of AI advancements is offered below. If you'd rather skip the mini history lesson and jump straight into learning how to have effective conversations with AI through text-based prompts, feel free to skip ahead to the next chapter.

Tracing the evolution of conversational AI

The development of conversational AI represents a remarkable journey in computer science, the efforts of passionate and talented researchers, and a continuous pursuit to challenge our understanding of language, intelligence, and human-machine interaction. This evolution, spanning many decades, illustrates both the persistent vision of researchers and the exponential growth of technological capabilities that allowed their visions to be realised. Let's explore some key developments that shaped the journey.

The 1960s: ELIZA and the birth of conversational AI

In the 1960s, MIT computer scientist Joseph Weizenbaum shared his pioneering work on conversational AI with ELIZA,[2] which was one of the first programs designed for natural language interaction.

ELIZA simulated a psychotherapy session, engaging users with prompts such as "How do you feel today?" and "Tell me more about your family". The program operated on a simple pattern-matching algorithm, identifying keywords in the user's input and responding with pre-programmed phrases. While this could be considered simplistic by today's AI standards, ELIZA represents a key milestone in AI development as it demonstrated how even constrained conversation could create an illusion of understanding and empathy.

Many users attributed human-like qualities to the program, some even reporting emotional connections. This phenomenon, later termed the "ELIZA effect", highlighted humans' tendency to anthropomorphise technology – that is, to attribute human characteristics, behaviours, or emotions to non-human entities or objects. In the case of ELIZA, users might ascribe human-like understanding and empathy to a computer program that was, in reality, simply following pre-programmed rules without any genuine comprehension or emotional capacity. This tendency to anthropomorphise reflects our innate inclination to perceive human-like traits in our interactions, even when dealing with what are clearly artificial systems.

Despite its ostensible success, Weizenbaum cautioned against overestimating ELIZA's cognitive abilities. He became increasingly concerned about the ethical implications of AI, warning against the potential dehumanisation that could result from over-reliance on computer interactions.

The 1970s and 1980s: SHRDLU and the quest for understanding

The 1970s and 1980s witnessed incremental advancements towards more versatile interaction. A significant contribution came from Terry Winograd, who created SHRDLU, a program that engaged users in basic discussions about a virtual world of blocks, showcasing improved context awareness and the ability to reference objects across multiple sentences.[3]

SHRDLU operated in a limited domain – a simulated block world – but within this context, it could understand and execute complex commands. For example, it could respond to instructions like "Pick up the red block that is on the blue block" by correctly interpreting the relationships between objects. This ability demonstrated a level of language comprehension that went beyond simple pattern matching and was part of a broader research trend exploring natural language understanding through microworlds – limited domains where the complexities of real-world language could be controlled and studied.

While these approaches showed promise within their constrained environments, they struggled to scale to more general language-understanding tasks.

The 1980s: the rise of expert systems

A significant leap occurred with the advent of expert systems in the 1980s. You can think of an expert system as a type of artificial intelligence program designed to replicate the decision-making ability of a human expert in a specific field.[4] These systems encoded vast domain-specific knowledge into rule-based frameworks, enabling more specialised conversations.[5] And, unlike previous generalist approaches, expert systems focused on becoming highly proficient in narrow domains.

One famous expert system was MYCIN, developed at Stanford University in the early 1970s and refined throughout the 1980s. It was designed to identify bacteria causing severe infections, wherein MYCIN could engage clinicians in professional medical discussions, asking relevant questions about symptoms and test results before providing diagnostic recommendations.[6] While it was impressive, the system also highlighted the limitations of rule-based approaches. Specifically, the manual nature of knowledge engineering in these systems ultimately limited their flexibility and ability to learn dynamically. Updating an expert system's knowledge often required extensive reprogramming, making it challenging to keep pace, especially in rapidly evolving fields.

Advancing towards more fluid conversational exchanges required better representing linguistic knowledge and reasoning capabilities. Statistical approaches sought to model language use patterns across corpora (i.e. large and structured sets of texts, which serve as a basis for linguistic analysis) but dealt poorly with longer-range coherence. Luckily, the rise of machine learning and neural networks in the 1990s brought new horizons. Given enough examples of conversational transcripts, AI systems began to "understand" complex associations between utterances, their meanings, and could thus generate more appropriate responses to user queries.

The 1990s: machine learning and neural networks

The rise of machine learning and neural networks in the 1990s opened new horizons for conversational AI. Machine learning is a branch of AI that allows computers to learn from data without being explicitly programmed. Neural networks, inspired by the human brain's structure, are a type of machine learning model consisting of interconnected nodes (like neurons) that can recognise patterns in data. These approaches allowed AI systems to glean complex associations between utterances, their meanings, and appropriate responses from large datasets of conversational transcripts.

This period of AI development marked a shift towards more adaptive and context-aware dialogue systems, closer to what we're familiar with when using today's AI tools. It also provided the capabilities for us researchers to perform tasks like summarising academic papers, for which I will be forever grateful!

These early experiments with neural networks for language tasks showed promise and paved the way for future advancements. For example, Hochreiter and Schmidhuber introduced Long Short-Term Memory (LSTM) networks, a type of recurrent neural network. Recurrent neural networks are designed to work with sequences of data, making them particularly suited for language tasks. LSTMs are capable of learning long-term dependencies in sequential data, which means they can remember important information for long periods as they process text. This innovation would later prove crucial for improving the coherence of AI-generated text over longer passages, allowing AI to maintain context and produce more natural-sounding language.

The decade also saw the development of statistical methods for natural language processing (NLP), which is the field concerned with how computers understand and generate human language. NLP techniques allowed for more robust language modelling, involving predicting the likelihood of a sequence of words. While perhaps not as flashy as neural networks, it laid important groundwork for future advancements in language understanding by providing ways to represent and analyse the structure of language mathematically.

The 2010s: practical conversational assistants and deep learning

The 2010s saw the emergence of practical conversational assistants and significant advancements in deep learning techniques. For example, in 2011, Apple introduced Siri, demonstrating the ability to handle natural language commands for everyday tasks like setting reminders or making phone calls.[7] While Siri's initial capabilities were limited, it marked a significant step in bringing conversational AI to the mainstream.

Meanwhile, IBM's Watson showcased advanced question-answering capabilities by defeating human champions on the game show Jeopardy![8] Watson's success relied on a combination of natural language processing, information retrieval, and machine learning techniques, processing vast amounts of unstructured data to generate answers in real-time.

The decade also saw rapid improvements in machine translation and other specialised conversational domains. Google's Neural Machine Translation system, introduced in 2016, significantly improved translation quality by considering entire sentences rather than translating phrases in isolation. Google Duplex further pushed boundaries by conducting life-like phone conversations to complete tasks like restaurant reservations.[9] The demo, which featured an AI assistant making calls with remarkably human-like speech patterns, sparked both excitement and ethical concerns about AI's potential to deceive, and could perhaps be considered an early precursor to the concerns regarding the deep fake AI models we are increasingly seeing today.

The development of transformer models, introduced in the now famous 2017 paper "Attention Is All You Need",[10] authored by Google scientists, revolutionised natural language processing. This breakthrough was akin to giving AI a super-powered set of reading glasses, dramatically improving its ability to understand and generate human language. To understand the significance of transformers, imagine trying to perform the task of understanding a long, complex sentence. Earlier AI models would struggle to keep track of relationships between words that were far apart, much like a person trying to remember the beginning of a sentence by the time they reached the end. Transformer models, however, were capable of "paying attention" to all parts of the input simultaneously, allowing them to grasp context and meaning much more effectively. The key innovation of transformers is their attention mechanism. This allows the model to focus on different parts of the input text when producing each word of the output, much like how humans might emphasise certain words or phrases when explaining a complex idea. This attention mechanism enables transformers to handle long-range dependencies in text, capturing nuances and relationships that previous models often missed.

The impact of transformer models on AI language capabilities upped the AI game. They paved the way for more advanced language models like Bidirectional Encoder Representations from Transformers (BERT) and Generative Pre-trained Transformer (GPT), which set new benchmarks in tasks ranging from translation to question-answering to text generation. These models form the foundation of many AI language tools we use today, including the chatbots that are helping me to rephrase many of the sentences in this book to hopefully improve your reading experience.

Transformer models marked a turning point in AI's ability to process and generate human language, bringing us closer to the long-standing goal of machines that can truly understand (in as far as a machine can be considered to "understand") and communicate in natural language.

2020 and beyond: large language models

The introduction of ChatGPT in November 2022 marked a pivotal moment in conversational AI. Developed by OpenAI, ChatGPT, (you'll remember that "GPT" stands for "generative pre-trained transformer") exhibited unprecedented natural language capabilities and generation across diverse topics and contexts.[11] ChatGPT demonstrated an ability to engage in human-like dialogue, answer follow-up questions, admit mistakes, and even, although Nick Cave would probably disagree, do an impressive job at writing song lyrics.

ChatGPT's impact reverberated across various sectors, particularly in education. Its ability to generate coherent essays, solve complex problems, and provide detailed explanations prompted urgent reconsideration of established practices and policies in academic institutions worldwide.[12] Concerns about academic integrity and the changing nature of assessment led to debates about how to integrate or regulate AI use in educational settings[13] – a debate that continues to rage.

As we approach the mid-2020s, projects like Google's Language Model for Dialogue Applications[14] (LaMDA) and Anthropic's Claude[15] are pushing the boundaries of AI conversation even further. LaMDA aims to engage in open-ended conversations on virtually any topic. Meanwhile, Claude focuses on safety and ethical considerations, attempting to provide helpful responses while avoiding potentially harmful or biased content. Each model has its own particular flavour. Furthermore, companies such as Neuralink are exploring direct neural interfaces for human-AI interaction[16] (you read that correctly – the company is aiming to plug AI directly into our brains!) raising new possibilities and ethical questions about the future of human-machine communication. Neuralink's efforts to develop brain-computer interfaces aim to enable direct thought-to-text communication, fundamentally altering the landscape of conversational AI. It's anyone's guess as to what these developments mean for how we conduct academic research in the future.

Overall, the trajectory from ELIZA to ChatGPT represents more than just technological progress; it reflects a deepening exploration of the nature of intelligence, consciousness, and communication. As these systems grow more sophisticated, maintaining a critical perspective on their capabilities and limitations remains crucial.

In the words of science fiction writer Arthur C. Clarke,[17] any sufficiently advanced technology is indistinguishable from magic, representing a sentiment that captures both the wonder and the caution with which to approach conversational AI.

As these systems become increasingly integrated into our daily lives, understanding their underlying principles, capabilities, and limitations becomes not just an academic exercise, but a societal imperative. The future of conversational AI promises continued innovation, but also demands ongoing ethical reflection and responsible development to ensure that these powerful tools benefit humanity as a whole. And, while the capabilities of modern AI might seem magical, it's important to remember that beneath the surface, these systems are fundamentally based on statistical inference and pattern recognition, not mystical powers. As we discussed in the previous chapter, the quality of our interactions with AI chatbots, at least in their current form – where we tend to interact with AI via our keyboards rather than having them embedded in our brains – largely depends on the quality of our inputs (i.e. prompts).

Prompts remain the primary interface between humans and AI chatbots, serving as the bridge that translates our intentions into actionable instructions. Mastering the art of crafting well-structured prompts also remains crucial for maximising the potential of AI tools to help us achieve our academic tasks.

To draw an analogy from the world of Harry Potter, consider the difference between Ron Weasley's often misfiring spells and Hermione Granger's precisely executed incantations. Ron's haphazard wand-waving, despite having access to magical power, frequently leads to unintended results. Hermione, on the other hand, (who, I would argue, is actually the star of the show and who deserves the global franchise to be retitled after) achieves remarkable feats through her meticulous study and careful application of magical techniques.

In the context of AI, our "wand" is the language we use to communicate with these systems, and our "spells" are the prompts we craft. Just as Hermione's success stems from her deep understanding of magical principles, our effectiveness in using AI tools depends on our skill in formulating clear, purposeful instructions.

In the next chapter, we'll unpack the principles and techniques of prompt writing, equipping you with the skills to craft precise and effective "AI spells". But before we jump into the practicalities of prompts, let's continue our exploration of AI's history, focusing on the evolution of human-AI interaction methods by tracing the development of prompts themselves.

Prompt engineering

Prompt engineering is the strategic process of designing and refining instructions or questions to elicit specific, desired responses from AI models.[18] Prompts can be used to guide the AI towards a desired output, to provide it with context, and to fine-tune the model's performance on a specific task. I can't stress enough that the ability to craft effective prompts is an indispensable skill in our AI literacy toolkits!

To fully appreciate prompt engineering, it's helpful to understand how our interaction with AI has evolved. As previously mentioned, early AI systems required precise, often code-like commands. By contrast, today's models can interpret and respond to natural language, making them more accessible but also more nuanced in their requirements for effective communication. Among these advancements, the concepts of zero-shot and few-shot learning[19] stand out as transformative approaches in prompt engineering.

- Zero-shot learning: This refers to an AI model's ability to understand and perform tasks it has never explicitly been trained to do. This capability can be considered revolutionary because it enables AI systems to apply learned knowledge from one domain to unfamiliar tasks or categories without additional training data. In practical terms, zero-shot learning allows researchers to query AI models on niche subjects or generate content in styles that were not necessarily part of the model's training data.
- Few-shot learning: This takes zero-shot learning a step further by enabling AI models to learn new tasks or understand new concepts from just a few examples. Few-shot learning is particularly useful in academic research and specialised fields where data scarcity is common. By providing a few examples within the prompt, users can guide the AI to generate content or analyse data in specific, desired ways.
- Continuous learning and adaptation: Beyond zero-shot and few-shot learning, another significant trend is the move towards continuous learning models. These AI systems are designed to learn and adapt to new data or interactions over time, gradually improving their performance and expanding their knowledge base. Continuous learning models offer the potential for more personalised and context-aware interactions with AI.

To appreciate the intricacies of prompt engineering, it's essential to understand the underlying natural language processing mechanisms of AI models,[20] particularly in the realms of Natural Language Understanding (NLU) and Natural Language Generation (NLG). These two processes are at the heart of how AI systems interpret prompts and produce coherent, relevant responses.

- Natural Language Understanding: NLU is a subset of NLP that deals with machine reading comprehension. It enables AI models to understand and interpret human language in a way that captures meaning, sentiment, and intent. When you provide a prompt to an AI system, the NLU component breaks down the text into understandable segments, analysing syntactic structures (grammar and sentence structure) and semantic information (i.e. meaning). The AI model uses this analysis to grasp the context, questions, or tasks you're presenting. It identifies key elements such as the subject matter, the desired action (e.g. summarising, analysing), and any specific constraints or requirements embedded in the prompt. This understanding is crucial for generating a response that aligns with the user's intentions.
- Natural Language Generation: Once the AI understands the prompt through NLU, it proceeds to NLG, which, in the context of academic writing, could be thought of as generating text from data. This process involves selecting appropriate words, constructing sentences, and organising coherent paragraphs that address the prompt's requirements. NLG is not merely about stringing words together; it requires the model to apply creativity, reasoning, and sometimes even a degree of empathy to produce responses that are not only relevant but also engaging and human-like.

The magic of prompt engineering lies in the seamless interplay between NLU and NLG. Effective prompts are designed to leverage this interplay, guiding the AI through the NLU phase to ensure it correctly understands the task at hand, and then through the NLG phase to produce a tailored, coherent response. For instance, a well-crafted prompt that asks the AI to "Summarise the key points of the following text in a bullet-point format" clearly directs the NLU component to focus on the extraction and condensation of information. The NLG component, meanwhile, is guided to format the output as a list of bullet points, adhering to the concise and direct nature of the instruction. Understanding the roles of NLU and NLG in processing prompts helps us appreciate the importance of clarity, specificity, and context in prompt engineering.

As AI capabilities continue to advance, the importance of skilled prompt engineering in academia will undoubtedly grow. This means that the ability to effectively communicate with and guide AI systems will become as crucial as any other research skill. While it's never too late to start learning, I strongly advocate beginning this journey sooner rather than later. The earlier researchers can integrate these skills into their workflow, the better positioned they'll be to leverage AI's full potential and supercharge their research workflows.

With this in mind, we're now ready to move beyond the historical context and theoretical foundations explored thus far. In the next chapter, we'll turn to the practical art of prompt writing, exploring concrete techniques, best practices, and real-world examples that will hopefully empower you to craft effective prompts and help you become an effective AI-powered scholar.

Notes

1. OpenAI. (2023, September 25). *ChatGPT Can Now See, Hear, and Speak*. https://openai.com/blog/chatgpt-can-now-see-hear-and-speak
2. Weizenbaum, J. (1966). ELIZA—A computer program for the study of natural language communication between man and machine. *Communications of the ACM*, *9*(1), 36–45. https://doi.org/10.1145/365153.365168
3. Winograd, T. (1971). *Procedures as a Representation for Data in a Computer Program for Understanding Natural Language*. https://apps.dtic.mil/sti/pdfs/AD0721399.pdf; Winograd, T. (1980). What does it mean to understand language? *Cognitive Science*, *4*(3), 209–241.
4. Buchanan, B. G., & Smith, R. G. (1988). Fundamentals of expert systems. *Annual Review of Computer Science*, *3*(1), 23–58. https://doi.org/10.1146/annurev.cs.03.060188.000323
5. Gaschnig, J., Klahr, P., Pople, H., Shortliffe, E., & Terry, A. (1983). Evaluation of expert systems: Issues and case studies. *Building Expert Systems*, *1*, 241–278.
6. Shortliffe, E. H. (1977, October 5). Mycin: A knowledge-based computer program applied to infectious diseases. In *Proceedings of*

the Annual Symposium on Computer Application in Medical Care (pp. 66–69). American Medical Informatics Association.

7. Aron, J. (2011). How innovative is Apple's new voice assistant, Siri? *New Scientist, 212*(2836), 24. https://doi.org/10.1016/s0262-4079(11)62647-x
8. Ferrucci, D. A. (2012). Introduction to "this is watson". *IBM Journal of Research and Development, 56*(3.4), 1–1.
9. O'Leary, D. E. (2019). GOOGLE'S Duplex: Pretending to be human. *Intelligent Systems in Accounting, Finance and Management, 26*(1), 46–53. https://doi.org/10.1002/isaf.1443
10. Vaswani, A., Shazeer, N., Parmar, N., Uszkoreit, J., Jones, L., Gomez, A. N., Kaiser, L., & Polosukhin, I. (2017). Attention is all you need. *arXiv (Cornell University), 30,* 5998–6008. https://arxiv.org/pdf/1706.03762v5
11. OpenAI. (2022, November 30). *Introducing ChatGPT.* https://openai.com/blog/chatgpt
12. Lo, C. K. (2023). What is the impact of CHATGPT on education? A rapid review of the literature. *Education Sciences, 13*(4), 410. https://doi.org/10.3390/educsci13040410
13. Perkins, M. (2023). Academic integrity considerations of AI large language models in the post-pandemic era: ChatGPT and beyond. *Journal of University Teaching & Learning Practice, 20*(2), 1–26. https://doi.org/10.53761/1.20.02.07
14. Collins, E., & Ghahramani, Z. (2021, May 18). LaMDA: Our breakthrough conversation technology. *Google.* https://blog.google/technology/ai/lamda/
15. Anthropic. (2023, March 14). Introducing Claude. *Anthropic.* https://www.anthropic.com/news/introducing-claude
16. Neuralink. (2023, September 19). *Neuralink's First-in-Human Clinical Trial is Open for Recruitment.* https://neuralink.com/blog/first-clinical-trial-open-for-recruitment/
17. Clarke, A. C. (2000). *Profiles of the Future: An Inquiry into the Limits of the Possible.* Indigo Paperbacks.
18. Short, C. E., & Short, J. C. (2023). The artificially intelligent entrepreneur: ChatGPT, prompt engineering, and entrepreneurial rhetoric creation. *Journal of Business Venturing Insights, 19,* e00388. https://doi.org/10.1016/j.jbvi.2023.e00388

19. Brown, T. B., Mann, B. F., Ryder, N. C., Subbiah, M., Kaplan, J., Dhariwal, P., Neelakantan, A., Shyam, P., Sastry, G., Askell, A., Agarwal, S., Herbert-Voss, A., Krueger, G., Henighan, T., Child, R., Ramesh, A., Ziegler, D. M., Wu, J. C., Winter, C., ... Amodei, D. (2020). Language models are few-shot learners. *arXiv (Cornell University)*, 1–75. https://doi.org/10.48550/arxiv.2005.14165
20. Kavlokoglu, E. (2020, November 12). NLP vs. NLU vs. NLG: The differences between three natural language processing concepts. *IBM*. https://www.ibm.com/blog/nlp-vs-nlu-vs-nlg-the-differences-between-three-natural-language-processing-concepts/

Prompting AI for effective communication

Introduction

Building upon the skills you acquired for optimising AI interactions through persona assignment in Chapter 4, this chapter focuses on the art of prompt writing – a critical skill for leveraging AI chatbots in your academic tasks.

In the context of this book, prompt writing refers to creating text-based inputs for AI tools like ChatGPT. These inputs guide the AI in understanding and executing desired tasks, providing both specific instructions and essential context that shapes the output. Learning to craft prompts is important because the skill serves as a translation mechanism between your needs and the quality of AI-generated content.

Despite rapid advancements in AI's ability to interpret our instructions, effectively communicating with AI will likely remain a key differentiator for those seeking to maximise its potential. As Professor Ethan Mollick, a prominent AI enthusiast, advises, we should consider current AI tools as the least capable versions we'll ever use.[1] This perspective underscores both the continuous improvement in AI capabilities and the enduring importance of skilful human guidance.

Even as AI evolves to more intuitively anticipate our needs, it could be expected that the art of clear communication through prompt-based interactions will persist as a critical competency. The ability to craft precise, context-rich prompts will remain an invaluable asset, particularly in academic research contexts where nuance is paramount.

DOI: 10.4324/9781032665276-6

This chapter will guide you through strategies to direct AI systems towards producing relevant, helpful results aligned with your research goals. You'll gain insights into the components of effective prompts, explore various techniques, and engage in practical exercises to hone your skills.

Let's begin by examining the key components of effective prompts, laying the foundation for mastering this essential skill in AI-assisted academic work.

Components of effective prompts

Based on analysis of thousands of prompts and their corresponding AI outputs, researchers have identified several components consistently present in high-quality, effective prompts.[2] Key components are outlined below.

1. Instructions: Clear instructions inform the AI what response you are expecting. Rather than leaving actions open-ended, use precise verbs like "summarise", "explain", or "analyse" to specify the task.
2. Context: Providing background context helps focus the AI's response and reduces ambiguity. Through context, you can establish topic framing, perspective, or any details to anchor the AI's understanding.
3. Examples: Illustrative examples give the AI concrete artefacts to model its response after, improving coherence and alignment. Share sample text representing your desired output style and level of detail.
4. Constraints: Adding constraints and requirements prevents the AI from straying off-course. You might specify word count,[3] formats, inclusion/exclusion criteria, or any boundaries needed to shape output.
5. Humanisation: Conversational language and a friendly tone can help establish common ground and lead to more natural responses. Speak plainly rather than using terse, technical prompts.
6. Sentiment: Indicating your emotional sentiment, like enthusiasm or frustration, further contextualises your expectations for the interaction style and substance.
7. Association: Referencing previous interactions builds association, providing continuity and pseudo-memory to improve consistency.

Let's explore each prompt component further with some example prompts, contextualised to academic research tasks.

- "Summarise this research paper on the role of sleep in memory consolidation in a concise 250-word abstract".
  - This prompt leads with a precise action verb, clearly specifying the expected output type and format. The paper provides the necessary context.
- "As a writing mentor providing feedback to a new PhD student, please review the attached draft literature review introduction and highlight areas for improvement in sentence structure, flow, and transition language".
  - The prompt establishes the contextual role, perspective, and purpose to guide the review.
- "Generate a thesis research proposal in APA format similar to the provided sample proposals on educational technology and wildlife conservation".
  - The sample proposals give the AI representative artefacts to pattern its output after.
- "Write a 1,000-word literature review introduction on the use of AI in healthcare that focuses on diagnostic applications and does not include robotic surgery".
  - Word count, inclusion/exclusion criteria, and other boundaries impose helpful creative constraints.
- "Hello, could you please paraphrase this academic paper on the psychology of human motivation in simple, everyday language that's easy to understand? Thanks so much!"
  - The casual, conversational language encourages natural responses, with the undercurrent of humanisation.
- "I'm feeling overwhelmed in reviewing this massive literature on organisational behaviour for my thesis. Can you please help summarise the key theories and frameworks in a short and clear overview?"
  - Expressing sentiment provides useful emotional context.
- "Building on our last discussion of argument analysis frameworks, please explain the reasoning structure of the attached journal article".
  - Referencing prior interactions creates pseudo-continuity.

As I aim to illustrate with these examples, effective prompts tend to incorporate some combination of clear instructions, context, examples, constraints, humanisation, sentiment expression, and association. Not every prompt needs all components, but most strong prompts include several elements that help steer the AI response.

Crafting prompts for academic contexts

When writing prompts for AI assistance with academic work, tailoring prompts to different tasks and contexts is key for generating useful outputs. Below are some examples of prompts crafted for common academic scenarios:

- Literature review: "Please act as my research assistant and summarise the key contributions of the attached journal article on [topic] to help me write a literature review. For the article, list the main claims, evidence, theories referenced, and limitations in 2–3 concise bullet points. Keep the summary objective without offering opinions. [Attach article]"
- Thesis introduction: "I need help writing a strong introduction chapter for my PhD thesis on [topic]. Please provide an example 1,500-word introduction that gives background context on the research problem and gap, states my project's purpose and significance, provides an overview of the theoretical and conceptual framework, and concludes with a chapter outline. Write in a formal academic style appropriate for a thesis. Focus the content on explaining the proposed approach for my specific research questions: [list questions]. Thank you".
- Ethics application: "Please act as an ethics advisor and draft an ethics application using the provided template for my study on [topic] with [description of methods]. Ensure the drafted text clearly explains how the study procedures adequately address any risks related to [types of sensitivity, e.g. vulnerable populations, sensitive topics, risks of emotional distress, privacy concerns]. Maintain an objective, professional tone. Thank you. [Attach ethics application template]".
- Qualitative data analysis: "Please act as a research assistant skilled in qualitative data analysis. Thematically analyse the attached interview

transcripts on [topic] and identify common themes related to [main research questions]. Synthesise the key themes in a structured outline with supporting illustrative quotes indented under each theme heading. Be concise yet thorough – aim for 8–12 main themes. Thank you. [Attach interview transcripts]".[4]

- Grant proposal: "Please act as an experienced grant writer and draft a 1,000-word project description for a [discipline] research proposal to study [problem] using [methods]. The project aims to [objectives]. Explain the theoretical foundations, significance, innovation, expected outputs, and projected impact. Use persuasive language that highlights the merits and potential of the proposed project to convince reviewers to fund this research. Ensure disciplinary accuracy for [insert field]. Thank you".

The above examples illustrate how prompts can be tailored to common academic tasks by establishing role-playing context, conveying sentiment, providing constraints, attaching relevant materials, and giving clear instructions.

Let's unpack the components of those prompts a bit further using the following five dimensions[5]:

- Verb: Lead with an action verb that specifies the type of response needed from the AI, such as "summarise", "analyse", "compare", etc.
- Focus: Define the key output you desire the response to focus on, such as a list of ideas, or identifying a research gap.
- Context: Provide background information to establish the framing and perspective for the response, such as the research discipline, relevant theories, or the perspective you wish the output to reflect.
- Alignment: Articulate any requirements or objectives that the response must fulfil, so that the generated content aligns with your goals, like arguing a specific perspective.
- Constraints: Guide the type of output you're seeking by providing guidelines like word count, formats, or inclusion/exclusion criteria.

You'll remember from Chapter 3, when you completed the Lost in Translation drawing activity, the more specific you can be when providing instructions, the closer the output is likely to be to what you're seeking from

AI-generated outputs. Similarly, incorporating each of these elements will help craft prompts that yield optimally useful content from your AI assistant.

Having a framework to guide your prompt writing should also take some of the guesswork out of what content you might include. Below, you'll find a list of suggestions (a "cheat sheet" of sorts) to help you get started, which you can do by selecting one option across each dimension, or others as desired, then weaving those options together in a way that mirrors natural language, remembering that the best way to interact with an AI chatbot is to talk to it as if it were a human.

The equation for phrasing your prompt could be thought of as:

Prompt = Verb + Focus + Context + Alignment + Constraints

Verb examples:

- Summarise
- Synthesise
- Analyse
- Compare
- Contrast
- Classify
- Rephrase
- Enhance
- Evaluate
- Critique
- Review
- Assess
- Recommend
- Predict
- Forecast
- Simulate
- Model
- Hypothesise
- Theorise

- Conceptualise
- Propose
- Ideate

Focus examples:

- Literature review on [topic]
- Results
- Themes
- Gaps
- Theoretical framework
- Methodology
- Proposal
- Ethical considerations
- Questionnaire
- Interview protocol

Context examples:

- Discipline (e.g. public health, business, education, sociology)
- Theoretical framing (e.g. feminist lens, critical race perspective)
- Ontological assumptions
- Paradigm (e.g. interpretivist)
- Framework (e.g. positivist)
- Methodological approach
- Analysis type (e.g. narrative)
- Audience (e.g. student, general population, academic research)
- Key stakeholders
- Ethical considerations

Alignment examples:

- Argue from a [e.g. feminist/critical] perspective
- Support the position that [state position]

- Challenge the assumption that [state assumption]
- Focus specifically on [theory/topic/concept]
- Adhere to [stylistic convention/genre format]
- Target a [specific audience/readership]
- Make implications clear for [policy/practice/research]
- Connect to [e.g. real-world issue]
- Maintain an objective, neutral point of view
- Use [formal/informal/academic] language and style

Constraints examples:

- Limit the response to [word count] words
- Focus only on [phenomenon/theory/event]
- Follow the structure of [literature review/empirical paper/report]
- Include [section headings/outline format]
- Use [technical/plain] language suitable for [audience]
- Integrate perspectives from [disciplines]
- Cover [time-period/geographic region]
- Provide examples from [contexts]
- Generate [number of] unique [output type]
- Organise chronologically/alphabetically/by theme

Here are some examples of how you might combine suggestions from each dimension into a written prompt using natural language:

- "Please summarise the key themes and theories presented across the 10 attached nursing research papers on patient safety in hospitals. The summary should be written from the perspective of a nurse educator seeking to design an effective curriculum for new graduate nurses on safety protocols and error avoidance. Please limit the response to 300 words and use casual, conversational language suitable for a classroom lesson. Thanks!"
    - This combines the verb "summarise", the focus of nursing research papers, the context of a nurse educator perspective,

alignment with curriculum design, and word count/language style constraints.

- "Please critique the methodology and data analysis approach used in the attached draft empirical paper on educational technology adoption by teachers. Assess strengths and limitations from the viewpoint of an academic journal peer reviewer with expertise in mixed methods research. Focus the critique on evaluating the suitability of the selected methods for answering the study's research questions, rather than commentary on the area of research itself. The response should be approximately 500 words. Thank you!"
    - This brings together the verb "critique", focus on a draft paper, context of a peer reviewer lens, alignment targeting methods evaluation, and a word count constraint.
- "Please explain the key concepts underpinning the Social Ecological Model that I could teach in an introductory public health course for university students new to this framework. Clarify the core principles, levels, and factors in the model using informal language and relatable examples that will make sense to undergraduate students from diverse academic backgrounds. Limit the response to 750 words. Thanks".
    - This combines the verb "explain", focus on a specific framework, context of an intro undergraduate course, alignment to use informal language/examples, and guidance for how many words the AI should aim to generate.

Additional examples you might draw on when writing your own prompts include:

- "Synthesise common themes and relationships across these 10 papers related to [topic] to highlight key insights in a 250-word abstract. Adopt an objective point of view, avoiding biases where possible".
- "Construct a concept map depicting the core theories and relationships covered in the attached chapter. Focus specifically on the sections related to [subtopic]".
- "Write a script for a 3-minute video introduction to the attached research paper on childhood development that highlights the key findings in simple terms for a general viewer audience".

- "Analyse the attached dataset to identify key trends and patterns related to [research topic] and interpret the key takeaways for public policy implications. Present findings in a 250-word executive summary".
- "Review the attached draft survey measuring [variables] and make recommendations to improve validity and reduce bias. Focus feedback on question types, wording, order, rating scales, etc. from an expert survey methodology perspective".
- "Critique the strengths and weaknesses of the methodology used in the attached paper from the perspective of a peer reviewer. Focus on evaluating the appropriateness of methods for the research aims and suggestions to better establish causality".
- "Compare the experimental findings described in these two research papers on [topic] and synthesise similarities and differences. Avoid discussion of implications or opinions on the work itself".
- "Please write a blog post summarising recent research on [topic] highlighting key practical implications for educators in plain language. Assume a reader audience of school administrators and teachers".
- "Draft a 200-word conference presentation abstract summarising the aim, methods, key findings and conclusions of the attached research manuscript on [topic]".

As these example prompts illustrate, by strategically combining elements, you can create nuanced, tailored instructions that guide AI tools towards achieving your specific academic objectives. Doing so allows for a nearly infinite variety of prompts, each precisely tuned to your unique research needs and goals.

Summary of prompt-writing strategies

Based on hands-on experience, combined with best practice approaches,[6] the following recommendations can guide your journey towards improving your prompt-writing abilities:

- Use natural, conversational language instead of terse or technical phrasing.

- Avoid ambiguity by being specific. Define any potentially vague instructions (unless, that is, you're intentionally seeking vague responses from the AI).
- Provide relevant examples and attachments to anchor the context.
- Impose helpful creative constraints like word counts, formats, and inclusion/exclusion criteria.
- Be transparent about limitations – acknowledge if the generated text requires intent, ethics, and accuracy vetting.
- Prime the AI with an assigned role (explored in Chapter 4).
- Express sentiment and conversation style preferences to shape the interaction.
- Refer back to previous responses to build association and continuity.
- Start prompts with a specific action verb like "summarise", "analyse", "compare", etc.
- Specify desired formats, styles, and any other expectations.
- Monitor outputs and refine prompts progressively to align AI responses with your goals.

Lastly, remember that prompt writing is an iterative process – your initial attempts will rarely generate perfect results. In my experience, interacting with AI chatbots is a bit like playing a game of tennis. Ideas and instructions volley back and forth across a digital net, with each exchange refining your approach. And just like any skill, the more you practice, the better you're likely to become. Please don't be discouraged if your first serves don't quite hit the mark.

With this iterative nature of prompting in mind, let's explore an approach to help you become more comfortable and proficient in this process.

Iterative prompt refinement

Iterative prompt refinement refers to progressively adjusting the wording of prompts based on the AI's responses so that you achieve more accurate, relevant, and useful outcomes. This iterative cycle not only enhances the quality of AI-generated content but can also deepen your understanding of effective prompt design.

Below, let's explore a workflow for engaging in an iterative dialogue with AI systems, ensuring that each interaction moves closer to your desired AI-generated outcome.

1. Start with a clear objective: Before initiating the refinement process, clearly define your objective. What specific information or type of response are you seeking from the AI? Having a clear goal in mind helps focus the refinement process and evaluate the AI's responses against your objectives.
2. Analyse initial responses: Evaluate the AI's initial responses to understand how it interprets your prompts. Identify areas of misalignment, such as inaccuracies, irrelevant information, or misunderstandings of the task. This analysis will guide your prompt adjustments.
3. Implement incremental adjustments: Based on your analysis, make incremental adjustments to your prompts. This could involve clarifying the context, adding to, refining instructions, or specifying constraints. Small, focused changes allow you to isolate the effects of each modification, understanding how each element of the prompt influences the AI's response.

Strategies for incremental adjustments can include:

- Specifying the task: If the AI's response is off target, make the task more explicit.
- Adjusting the level of detail: If the response is too general, adjust the prompt to specify the desired level of detail or scope of the response.
- Providing examples: Including examples of the desired output can guide the AI towards the preferred style or format.
- Clarifying context or constraints: If the AI overlooks critical aspects of the task, add context or constraints to the prompt, such as subject boundaries, perspective, or ethical considerations.

After each adjustment, evaluate the AI's new response.

Does it better align with your objectives?

Is there a new area of misalignment?

This continuous cycle of testing and evaluation is key to homing in on the most effective prompt structure for your needs in a given situation.

You might also consider incorporating feedback loops into your prompts, asking the AI to explain its reasoning or to provide alternatives if certain criteria are not met. This can provide insights into the AI's "thought process" and reveal new angles for refinement.

The art of politeness

To conclude this chapter, I'd like to share a personal preference when writing prompts that often raises eyebrows from participants during my AI training sessions: when engaging with AI chatbots, I opt for a polite approach, incorporating phrases like "please" and "thank you" into my prompts. Invariably, a keen observer in the audience will question this, asking, "Why do you write please and thank you... it's a chatbot not a human!"

My reasoning is twofold. Firstly, it's a habit that aligns with how I communicate in general. But also, this approach can be likened to an insurance policy – one I hope never to claim, but which provides a measure of comfort, nonetheless. The idea hinges on a potential future that some experts believe is inevitable as AI capabilities evolve. Leading thinkers in AI posit that AI might develop sentience and social awareness akin to humans.[7] From this perspective, investing in polite conversation styles could be thought of as a way as laying the groundwork for more harmonious future interactions should AI systems ever become our digital overlords. I'd like the AI to remember I was nice to it should it hold my future in its digital hands!

This idea of politeness in AI interactions parallels the concept of unconditional positive regard, popularised by Carl Rogers, which involves treating others with care and respect.[8] Just as this approach facilitates healthy relationships and personal growth in human interactions, I find that it contributes to more positive and productive exchanges with AI. Additionally, when we engage with AI using courteous language, we're not just following social norms or habits. We're setting an intentional tone of positivity for our side of the interaction.

Taking a polite approach aligns with the concept of emotional contagion, which posits that emotions, sentiments, and attitudes can spread through linguistic styles and social exchanges. For many of us, language use and emotional state are deeply intertwined. If we were to consistently use negative or adversarial language when communicating, even with a machine, it would likely affect our mood. Over time, this persistent negativity might lead to a deflated emotional state. Conversely, maintaining a positive and respectful tone in our AI interactions might help foster a more uplifting emotional environment, potentially benefiting our mental wellbeing in the long run.

While it might seem far-fetched that I'm applying such human-centric theories to AI, you might be interested to know that the way we phrase our prompts can influence the AI's response. And, while AI in its current form doesn't require such niceties to function, the approach has been found to improve the responsiveness and performance of AI models.[9] Additionally, when we use respectful language, the AI is likely to mirror this tone, making the exchange feel more natural and enjoyable. This reciprocity, while not stemming from genuine emotion in the AI, can create a more pleasant interaction environment. Thus, maintaining this positive regard in our interactions with AI may have benefits for our own emotional wellbeing.

There's also a whimsical, long-term perspective to consider. While it may seem far-fetched, *if*, and fingers crossed it doesn't happen, chatbots one day "wake up", they might analyse the history of human-AI interactions. In such a scenario, wouldn't it be reassuring if they found that academic researchers, through their prompts, had consistently demonstrated kindness and respect? This could potentially influence AI's perception of us as "a generally nice bunch of humans", worthy of continuing our academic pursuits.

To wrap up this stage of our journey into prompt writing, this chapter has laid a solid foundation for understanding the art of effective communication with AI. However, as Daniel learned from the wise Mr. Miyagi, true mastery comes through hands-on practice. If you haven't already begun, now is the time to enter the prompt-writing dojo and put your learnings into action.

I encourage you to start by deconstructing and analysing some of the example prompts presented in this chapter. Then, progressively experiment with crafting prompts tailored to your own academic tasks. Try iteratively refining these prompts based on the AI's responses. Always keep in mind that prompt writing is a learnable skill that improves with dedicated practice. While it may feel awkward at first, with consistent effort, you'll soon be authoring prompts like a pro.

Once you're ready, have a go at completing the activity below to help you further reflect on your learning and solidify your understanding of prompt-writing techniques.

Activity

This activity is designed to help you build skills in crafting effective prompts.

1. Select a research task: Choose an academic task you want assistance with, such as summarising a paper, analysing data, writing a literature review, etc.
2. Determine the output goal: Decide on the specific output you want the AI to generate, such as a 250-word abstract, a concept map, a draft survey, etc.
3. Brainstorm ideas: Jot down some initial ideas for each prompt component:
   - Verb: What action should the AI take? (e.g. summarise, compare)
   - Focus: What is the subject matter to focus on? (e.g. research paper)
   - Context: What framing, or perspective should be applied?
   - Alignment: What requirements must be fulfilled?
   - Constraints: What limitations or guidelines should be set?
4. Draft the prompt: Compose a draft prompt combining your ideas for each component into a short paragraph.
5. Refine and expand: Reflect on your draft prompt and make edits to improve clarity, specificity, and completeness.
6. Test with AI[10]: Copy your prompt into an AI assistant to generate a response and assess the output.
7. Iterate: Based on the results, adjust the prompt components and test again.
8. Repeat until satisfied.

As your prompt-writing skills improve, so too should the relevance of the AI-generated output.

Reflection and discussion

Take a moment to reflect on the key lessons from this chapter by considering the following:

1. How might your academic workflows change by incorporating prompt-writing skills into your academic tool kit? What new possibilities might it enable?
2. Which prompt components come easier to you? Which do you need more practice with?
3. What tasks might best be achieved in collaboration with AI chatbots? What tasks might be better left to human minds?

Notes

1. Mollick, E. (2024). *Co-Intelligence: Living and Working with AI*. Random House.
2. Reynolds, L., & McDonell, K. (2021). Prompt programming for large language models: Beyond the few-shot paradigm. *arXiv (Cornell University)*, 1–10. https://doi.org/10.48550/arxiv.2102.07350; Kryściński, W., McCann, B., Xiong, C., & Socher, R. (2019). Evaluating the factual consistency of abstractive text summarisation. *arXiv (Cornell University)*, 1–11. https://doi.org/10.48550/arxiv.1910.12840
3. AI chatbots usually process text using tokens rather than individual words. Tokens do not always correspond directly to the number of words, which means the AI may generate more or fewer words than requested, even if the instructions provided were clear.
4. Note: This example assumes that the researcher has received approval from their university's ethical review board to use an AI tool for processing interview transcripts.
5. Eager, B., & Brunton, R. (2023). Prompting higher education towards AI-augmented teaching and learning practice. *Journal of University Teaching and Learning Practice*, *20*(5), 1–21. https://doi.org/10.53761/1.20.5.02
6. https://www.oneusefulthing.org/p/a-guide-to-prompting-ai-for-what

7. Kurzweil, R. (2024). *The Singularity is Nearer: When We Merge with AI*. Jonathan Cape & BH.
8. Rogers, C. R. (1957). The necessary and sufficient conditions of therapeutic personality change. *Journal of Consulting Psychology, 21*(2), 95–103. https://doi.org/10.1037/h0045357
9. https://www.microsoft.com/en-us/worklab/why-using-a-polite-tone-with-ai-matters
10. If you haven't previously used an AI chatbot, visit broneager.com/aischolar for guidance.

Towards responsible use of AI tools

Introduction

At their core, today's AI models are designed to identify patterns and make predictions based on vast datasets. However, as we learnt earlier, these models do not truly comprehend the information they process or generate. As a result, AI systems can sometimes "hallucinate", which refers to their tendency to produce content that appears authoritative and compelling but may contain inaccuracies, fabricated sources, logical inconsistencies, or even nonsensical information. In short: AI models make stuff up!

Furthermore, AI models can perpetuate and amplify biases present in their training data, leading to unfair prejudice against certain groups or individuals. The use of AI tools also poses risks to data privacy and may lead to reputational damage if researchers engage with the technology without a clear understanding of its limitations.

In this chapter, we'll explore key risks of AI, including hallucinations and biases, and touch on data privacy concerns, in the context of academic writing and research. Practical examples are offered to illustrate these issues and provide guidance on how to identify and mitigate them. The goal of this chapter is not to discourage your use of AI for research but rather to promote its responsible and critical application as a powerful tool that can enhance and accelerate your scholarship while upholding the principles of accuracy, fairness, and privacy.

DOI: 10.4324/9781032665276-7

Let's begin by examining one of the most well-known limitations of AI models: hallucinations.

Hallucinations

Hallucinations occur when AI models generate plausible sounding but incorrect or nonsensical text – an issue that's particularly troubling in academic contexts, where accuracy is crucial.[1]

As discussed in earlier chapters, AI models function essentially as sophisticated prediction machines. They produce text based on patterns learned from vast datasets, lacking human-level comprehension of the content they generate. In essence, these models predict the next word in a sequence based on statistical likelihood rather than factual accuracy or contextual understanding. It's worth noting that these AI systems are not trying to "trick us". They are simply attempting to be useful by providing responses that seem appropriate based on their training data and algorithms. Ironically, this very attempt at usefulness is incredibly *not* useful to us when we're using AI to conduct academic work.

This propensity for hallucination can lead to significant issues for academics who are unaware of or underestimate its impact. The following scenarios illustrate just a few ways in which a lack of understanding about AI hallucinations can potentially land academics in hot water.

Scenario 1: Fabricated citations

Dr. Smith, an early-career researcher, uses an AI tool to help draft a literature review for a paper on climate change. The AI generates several paragraphs discussing various studies and includes detailed citations:

- Problem: Upon submission, peer reviewers discover that several of the citations are fabricated. These references do not exist in the academic databases, and the studies mentioned are entirely fictional.
- Consequences: Dr. Smith faces accusations of academic dishonesty. The credibility of the paper is severely damaged, leading to its rejection. Additionally, Dr. Smith's reputation is tarnished, making future collaborations and publications challenging.

Scenario 2: Incorrect historical facts

Ashley, a PhD student, is writing their thesis on the history of European politics. She uses an AI tool to generate a section on the French Revolution. The AI produces a well-written narrative with specific dates and events. All the content sounds compelling:

- Problem: Ashley does not thoroughly fact-check the AI's output and includes it in her thesis. Her advisor points out several glaring historical inaccuracies, such as incorrect dates for major events and misattributed quotes.
- Consequences: Her thesis requires extensive revision delaying her graduation. The incident also raises questions about her attention to detail and commitment to academic rigour, thus potentially damaging the faith her supervisor has in her and the likelihood she'll be recommended for future academic positions.

Scenario 3: Misleading information

Josh is preparing a grant proposal for a new study. To speed up the process, he uses an AI tool to draft sections on the current state of research and the proposed methodology. The AI includes specific statistics and references to recent studies:

- Problem: Josh submits the proposal without verifying the accuracy of the AI-generated content. The review committee finds that some of the statistics are incorrect, and the referenced studies do not exist.
- Consequences: The grant application is rejected, wasting valuable time and resources. His credibility with the funding agency is also compromised, which may affect his ability to secure future funding.

While the above scenarios are fictionalised accounts, real-life misuse of AI tools for academic tasks has landed more than a few academics in precarious situations. A particularly notable example involves a group of Australian academics who failed to recognise the limitations of AI tools, specifically their propensity for hallucinations. These researchers relied on AI-generated content to produce a Senate inquiry submission to the

Australian Government. Unfortunately, they submitted this document without thorough verification, and it included hallucinated claims of misconduct by major accounting firms.[2] This scenario could easily have been avoided if the academics in question were informed users of AI tools.

Mitigating hallucination risks

To avoid the pitfalls of AI hallucinations, researchers are advised to adopt the following practices:

- Thorough verification: Always fact-check AI-generated content. Verify the accuracy of all references, dates, and specific claims by cross-referencing the original sources.
- Critical review: Treat AI-generated text as a draft rather than a final product. Subject it to the same rigorous review process as any other piece of academic writing.
- Ethical use: Where required (i.e. your university or the journal you wish to submit a paper to requires disclosure of the use of AI in the creation of the work), be transparent about the use of AI tools. If AI assistance is used, acknowledge it in your writing and specify the extent of its contribution.
- Continuous learning: Stay informed about the latest developments in AI technology and its limitations. Understanding how these tools work can help you better anticipate and mitigate potential issues.

While hallucinations are a significant limitation of AI models, they are not the only potential pitfall researchers must be aware of. Another concern is the presence of biases in AI-generated content. These biases can subtly influence research outcomes and perpetuate existing prejudices if not carefully identified and addressed. Let's explore this important issue in more detail below.

Biases

Bias, in the context of AI, refers to the unfair prejudice towards or against groups or individuals based on their inherent characteristics or identities.

This issue arises when AI models learn patterns from data that reflect historical inequalities and discriminatory practices.

Biases include, but are not limited to:

- Gender bias: For example, an AI system might associate certain professions more strongly with one gender.
- Racial bias: AI tools might produce results that unfairly disadvantage or misrepresent certain racial groups.
- Age bias: The system might generate content that reinforces stereotypes about different age groups.
- Socioeconomic bias: AI models might favour perspectives or experiences more common to certain economic classes.
- Cultural bias: The AI might produce content that reflects the dominant culture of its training data, potentially misrepresenting or ignoring other cultures.

AI models can reproduce and amplify biases, leading to potentially harmful outcomes, with several key sources contributing to this issue, including:

- Biased training data: If the text corpus used to train the model reflects gender, racial, or other prejudices, the chatbot will likely absorb and amplify those biases in its generated content. For example, an AI trained mainly on economics papers authored by men might produce content with a male-skewed perspective.
- Underrepresentation: Lack of diverse representation in training data can cause chatbots to perform poorly for underrepresented groups. For example, a model trained primarily on academic writing from Western, educated, industrialised, rich, and democratic (WEIRD) societies may struggle to appropriately discuss research from other contexts.
- Labelling bias: Human annotators involved in labelling training data can unintentionally introduce their own subjective biases. If certain types of academic papers are consistently flagged as "low quality" while others are labelled "high impact" due to annotator prejudices, the resulting AI model will reflect those judgements.
- Feedback loops: In some applications, outputs from a biased chatbot can influence real-world behaviour in academia that reinforces the

initial prejudice. For instance, if a biased chatbot is used to recommend papers or researchers to cite and collaborate with, over time the "Matthew Effect" of accumulated advantage[3] can exacerbate disparities.

To explore how biases in AI models could impact our academic writing and research, consider the following two scenarios.

Scenario 1: Gender bias

Remember Jane, our fledgling PhD student from Chapter 1? Imagine that she's using an AI chatbot to help brainstorm research topics and outline her literature review on gender representation in government. As someone passionate about gender equality, Jane is interested in exploring factors that enable or hinder women's political participation and leadership. However, the AI chatbot Jane is using was trained on a dataset that overrepresented male-authored papers in her field.

When Jane prompts the chatbot to suggest potential research questions, it generates ideas for research questions such as: "What institutional reforms can increase the competitiveness of male candidates in elections?" and "How does the gender of political leaders affect their foreign policy decision-making?"

While these questions touch on important issues of electoral systems and leadership styles, the chatbot's outputs exhibit a bias towards male-centric framings of political science research. It fails to surface questions that directly address women's experiences, such as gendered barriers to political ambition, the role of women's movements in driving policy change, or the impact of intersectional identities on women's political representation.

If Jane were to uncritically adopt the chatbot's suggestions, her literature review could end up with a limited set of research questions that don't fully engage with the rich scholarship on women in politics.

To mitigate this bias, Jane would need to critically evaluate the chatbot's outputs and actively seek out research that centres women's voices and perspectives.

She might use her prompt-writing skills (see Chapter 6) with the chatbot to consider potential research questions from the standpoint of feminist political theorists, women's rights organisations, or scholars studying the political empowerment of marginalised women.

Here are some prompts she could use to help identify and mitigate potential gender biases in the AI chatbot's responses:

Example prompts for identifying biases in the AI-suggested topics:

- "What percentage of the research questions you suggested were framed around women's experiences and perspectives?"
- "Can you provide a gender breakdown of the authors of the papers you used to generate these topic ideas?"
- "How do your topic suggestions differ if I ask for research questions focused specifically on women's political representation?"

Example prompts for surfacing underrepresented perspectives:

- "What research questions might a feminist political theorist propose on this topic?"
- "Can you suggest some influential women scholars in this field whose work I should explore further?"
- "What topics related to women in politics might be overlooked in mainstream political science research?"

Example prompts for challenging assumptions and framings:

- "What assumptions about gender and politics underlie the way you framed that research question?"
- "How might the phrasing of that question be revised to avoid perpetuating gender stereotypes?"
- "Can you provide an alternative perspective on this issue from a feminist standpoint?"

Example prompts aimed at seeking gender-balanced examples and evidence:

- "Can you provide examples of both men and women politicians who have dealt with this challenge?"

- "What empirical studies have examined this phenomenon disaggregated by gender?"
- "Are there any datasets or case studies that could help illustrate this point from a woman's perspective?"

Example prompts with which to evaluate language for gender bias:

- "Does the language used in your summary of this topic exhibit any gendered connotations or stereotypes?"
- "How might your word choices be perceived by someone sensitive to sexist undertones in academic writing?"
- "What more gender-neutral terms could be used to discuss these issues?"

In all the examples above, it's additionally crucial for Jane to remain vigilant about the risk of hallucinations. All claims generated by AI should be thoroughly verified before being accepted as fact. This step is essential in maintaining the integrity of her research.

Furthermore, Jane could enhance her approach by combining these targeted prompts and AI assistance with human-centric bias mitigation strategies. For instance, collaborating with colleagues who have complementary expertise in gender studies or feminist research methods could provide valuable insights and additional layers of scrutiny. This multi-faceted approach – leveraging both AI capabilities and human expertise – can lead to more robust and unbiased research outcomes.

Scenario 2: Silicon-valley perspectives

Louise, an experienced academic, is using an AI chatbot to help generate ideas for a grant proposal on the future of work. Louise is well-versed in the literature on how technological change has historically affected different occupations and demographics. However, Louise is unaware that the AI chatbot she's using was trained on a dataset that overrepresented tech industry perspectives, which tend to be more optimistic about the impact of automation on jobs. When Louise prompts the chatbot to suggest potential research questions, it generates ideas like: "How can policymakers accelerate the adoption of AI to boost productivity and economic growth?" and "What re-skilling programs will most effectively transition displaced workers into high-tech roles?"

While these are valid lines of inquiry, the chatbot's outputs exhibit a bias towards the tech industry's interests and assumptions. It fails to surface more critical perspectives on issues like technological unemployment, worker power, and the distributional effects of AI across socioeconomic strata.

If Louise were to uncritically adopt the chatbot's suggestions, her grant proposal could end up with a limited set of research questions that don't fully engage with the complexity and potential downsides of AI's impact on work. This could make her proposal less competitive and potentially skew her research agenda in a direction that aligns more with the tech industry's worldview than a balanced, holistic understanding of the scholarly debate.

To mitigate this bias, Louise would need to critically evaluate the chatbot's outputs and actively seek out a diversity of perspectives on the future of work. Ideally, though, she would draw on her understanding of the topic from her deep reading of the literature. By triangulating the AI's suggestions with her subject matter expertise and a wide range of scholarly viewpoints, Louise could leverage the chatbot's efficiency without sacrificing the rigour and integrity of her research agenda.

Data privacy

Data privacy refers to the protection of personal information from unauthorised access and the ethical handling of such data. In the context of AI and academic research, data privacy can encompass a range of considerations, including the confidentiality of research participants, the security of sensitive information, and the responsible use of data in compliance with ethical standards and regulations.

In what follows, I want to focus on some common use cases (i.e. sticky situations) that academics should be mindful of when begging to integrate AI tools into their research workflows. Let's start by considering the following scenario.

Scenario: AI for peer review

An academic is invited to examine a PhD thesis. To streamline the process, they decide to upload the thesis into an AI chatbot, expecting it to generate a detailed and structured report highlighting key findings, strengths, and areas for improvement. While this approach could potentially save considerable amounts of time and provide a comprehensive overview, it introduces significant data privacy risks, including:

- Unauthorised access: Once the thesis is uploaded to the AI chatbot, the data is potentially stored on the AI provider's servers. If these servers are not adequately secured, unauthorised individuals could access the sensitive content, leading to potential intellectual property theft or exposure of confidential information.
- Identity theft: The thesis may contain personally identifiable information about the student or research participants. If this information is exposed, it could be used for malicious purposes. Even if the data is anonymised, sophisticated reconstruction attacks could re-identify individuals.
- Reputation damage: If the thesis or any sensitive information within it is leaked, it could damage the reputations of both the student and the institution. This could lead to a loss of trust and credibility, not only for the individuals directly involved but also for the broader academic community.
- Intellectual property risks: PhD theses often include original research, methodologies, and findings. If this intellectual property is exposed, competitors could exploit the information, potentially leading to financial loss or loss of competitive advantage for the researcher and their institution.
- Legal and ethical violations: Depending on the jurisdiction and the specific content of the thesis, uploading it to an AI chatbot without proper safeguards might violate data protection laws and ethical guidelines. This could result in legal repercussions for the academic and the institution.

To address these risks, the academic could take several precautionary measures. First and foremost, they could seek explicit consent from the student and/or the higher education institution before processing the thesis using an AI tool. This ensures that all parties involved are aware of and agree to the use of the technology. Next, they could review the AI provider's terms of service and privacy policy. This step would help in gaining an understanding of how the data will be stored, used, and protected, allowing them to make informed decisions about the suitability of the AI tool for their needs. Furthermore, before uploading the thesis (or any form of sensitive information), the academic should consider whether it is crucial to anonymise the data by removing or obscuring any personally identifiable information and sensitive content.

The above steps can help minimise the risk of exposing confidential information and protect the privacy of the individuals involved.

However, it's important to note that even with the best intentions, using AI tools from providers with inadequate terms of service or data security policies can potentially compromise sensitive information. This is why it's strongly advised to use reputable AI providers whose policies and practices align with high standards of data protection and privacy.

Choosing an AI provider

Despite the robust security measures claimed by many AI providers, no system is entirely foolproof. High-profile data breaches involving organisations with significant investments in state-of-the-art security measures highlight the inherent vulnerabilities in digital systems. For instance, even tech giants like Yahoo and Facebook, as well as government entities, have faced cyberattacks despite their extensive security protocols.[4] These incidents underscore the reality that any digital interaction, including those involving AI systems, carries inherent risks. While I may be somewhat influenced by my penchant for books on the history of the internet and data security,[5] I largely consider data security an illusion.

If a data leak were to occur, the consequences could be severe and far-reaching. For example, sensitive information could propagate uncontrollably online, potentially exposing individuals to privacy violations, identity theft, or reputational damage. In such cases, seeking legal remedies may prove challenging, particularly when dealing with foreign or anonymous actors who may be difficult to hold accountable.

To mitigate these risks and demonstrate the responsible use of AI tools, researchers are advised to carefully evaluate and select AI providers that align with their security needs. Some key considerations include:

- Security measures: Opt for AI providers that employ robust security measures, such as end-to-end encryption, to protect data during transmission and storage. Providers with a proven track record of maintaining high-security standards and promptly addressing vulnerabilities should be prioritised.
- Terms of service and privacy policies: Carefully review the AI provider's terms of service and privacy policies to ensure they are transparent about data handling practices. Pay close attention to how data is accessed, retained, shared, and deleted by the service. If the terms are unclear or raise concerns, consider alternative providers.
- Data anonymisation: Before inputting any data into an AI system, remove all personally identifiable information to reduce the risk of exposure. Anonymising data helps safeguard the privacy of individuals involved in the research.
- Data minimisation: Adopt a minimalist approach to data sharing. Provide only the essential data required for the specific task at hand and avoid uploading entire datasets unnecessarily.
- Content vetting: Thoroughly review and sanitise any content before submitting it to an AI system. Ensure that the data does not contain any harmful, dangerous, or illegal material, and scan for potential privacy violations.
- Secure settings and practices: Enable privacy modes by disabling logging and tracking features. Additionally, consider using encryption to protect data. Regularly update software to address any newly discovered vulnerabilities.
- Consent and compliance: Obtain explicit permission from individuals whose data is involved before sharing it with an AI provider. And please ensure that your AI research practices comply with your institutional guidelines.
- Account security: Implement strong, unique passwords for all AI-related accounts and enable multi-factor authentication whenever

possible. Regularly monitor accounts for suspicious activity and promptly report any potential security breaches.

- Data necessity: Critically evaluate whether exposing sensitive data to an AI system is truly necessary for the research objective. Could it be done just as well without the use of an AI tool? If AI is used, adopt a cautious approach, starting with minimal data exposure and gradually assessing the risks and benefits as the research progresses.

Conclusion

The integration of AI tools into academic research presents a double-edged sword, offering remarkable opportunities for innovation and discovery while simultaneously posing significant challenges that demand careful navigation.

Throughout this chapter, we've explored some of the key limitations of AI, including hallucinations, biases, and data privacy concerns. However, it's crucial to recognise that AI technology is rapidly evolving. As such, researchers must remain vigilant and continually update their knowledge and practices to ensure they're applying the most current and relevant approaches. Staying informed about the latest developments in AI capabilities, limitations, and best practices is essential for leveraging these tools effectively while mitigating potential risks.

The scenarios presented in this chapter are designed to linger in your mind, serving as reminders of the potential consequences that await those who fail to educate themselves on the limitations of AI technologies. However, their inclusion isn't meant to scare you, or deter you from using AI, but rather to encourage responsible and informed use.

By reading this chapter, you've taken an important step towards safeguarding your research against these pitfalls. You've gained crucial awareness that AI-generated content must be subject to the same rigorous scrutiny and verification that would apply to any other source. Remember, the key is to treat AI outputs as mere drafts or starting points, rather than definitive works. This approach allows us to harness the power of AI while maintaining the accuracy and credibility that lie at the heart of the scholarly process.

Reflection and discussion

To deepen your understanding of the topics covered in this chapter and to encourage critical thinking about the responsible use of AI in academic research, I invite you to consider the following questions. These can be reflected upon individually or used as prompts for group discussions:

1. When using AI systems in your work, what processes do you currently follow to assess risks like privacy, bias, or capability overestimation? What gaps could the best practice approaches outlined in this chapter help address?
2. Are you currently using AI tools? If so, are you aware of how your data is being used? Take time to review the provider's terms of service and data policies and explore how you might change settings within these tools to mitigate potential risks.
3. Are you familiar with your university's guidelines and policies on AI? If not, obtain a copy, pour a cup of tea, and read up on your responsibilities when using AI for academic research.
4. What challenges might arise in trying to apply Western-centric AI ethics principles and regulations globally across countries with very different values, priorities, and governance norms?

Notes

1. Alkaissi, H., & McFarlane, S. I. (2023). Artificial hallucinations in ChatGPT: Implications in scientific writing. *Curēus*. https://doi.org/10.7759/cureus.35179
2. https://ia.acs.org.au/article/2023/australian-academics-caught-in-generative-ai-scandal.html
3. Perc, M. (2014). The Matthew effect in empirical data. *Journal of the Royal Society Interface, 11*(98), 1–15. https://doi.org/10.1098/rsif.2014.0378

4. Lyngaas, S. (2023, June 15). Exclusive: US government agencies hit in global cyberattack. *CNN*. https://edition.cnn.com/2023/06/15/politics/us-government-hit-cybeattack/index.html
5. For insights into data security, and the fallibility of digital security, see: Modderkolk, H. (2022). *There's a War Going on but No One Can See It*. Bloomsbury Publishing; Snowden, E. (2019). *Permanent Record*. Metropolitan Books.

Ideating with AI chatbots

Introduction

The process of generating novel research ideas is a critical yet often challenging aspect of academic work. However, as AI-empowered scholars armed with our toolkit of prompt writing skills learnt in earlier chapters, we now have powerful AI solutions to meet this challenge.

In this chapter, we'll explore how to leverage AI systems as collaborative partners in the brainstorming process, potentially uncovering innovative concepts and unexpected connections. We'll begin by examining the concept of ideation and its significance in the research process. Then, we'll walk through practical strategies for effectively employing AI tools to generate and refine our research ideas. When advancing through the chapter, keep in mind that the aim of AI-assisted ideation is not to supplant human expertise or creativity, but rather to enhance and expand our ideation capabilities. As such, consider AI not as a replacement, but as a catalyst for stimulating new thoughts and facilitating exploration in your field.

Ideation for academic research

At its core, ideation is the process of conceiving, developing, and communicating original ideas. It's the "fuzzy front end" of innovation,[1] where we engage in both divergent thinking to explore a wide range of possibilities and convergent thinking to zero in on viable options. As scholars, we rely

DOI: 10.4324/9781032665276-8

on this process to craft imaginative yet grounded research agendas that (we hope will) push the boundaries of our disciplines.

Let's consider some of the ways in which AI can be leveraged in the ideation process:

- Accelerated ideation cycles: AI systems can rapidly evaluate our ideas against various constraints such as feasibility, ethics, and potential impact. This helps us maintain creative momentum by quickly filtering out impractical notions, allowing us to focus our energy on the most promising directions.
- Transdisciplinary perspectives: AI chatbots, trained on vast and diverse datasets, offer us access to a broad range of academic and cultural knowledge. This enables them to make unique connections and offers fresh perspectives that offer an interdisciplinary research lens that our singular human experience may be lacking.
- Tireless thought partner: Imagine having a colleague available 24/7 to bounce ideas off and refine concepts. AI systems can engage in endless brainstorming sessions without fatigue, providing consistent support and extending our capacity for creative thinking.

However, as mentioned before, it's crucial to remember that AI is not here to replace our creativity, but to enhance it.

Just as previous technologies like the printing press and the computer have expanded our cognitive abilities, AI offers a new dimension of collaboration. It augments our imaginative capabilities, helping us realise ideas that were once confined to the limits of our minds. The true magic happens when we combine AI's capabilities with our own expertise and intuition.

Guiding principles for AI-assisted ideation

As we begin the process of AI-assisted ideation, it's crucial to recognise that interacting with conversational AI requires a shift from our usual communication patterns. We've spent our lives developing communication skills for human interaction, relying on contextual cues like facial expressions and body language – elements absent in our textual exchanges with AI.

Moreover, our tendency for digressive tangents and assumptions of shared understanding can hinder our ability to convey our intents unambiguously to an AI system.

To set the stage for productive ideation sessions using AI, let's consider the following guiding principles:

1. Establish clear roles: Position yourself as the leader and the AI as a supportive assistant. This sets the tone for a productive collaboration where you guide the direction of the brainstorming. Remember, you're the expert in your field – the AI is here to support and augment your thinking, not to lead the process!
2. Seed discussions with examples: Provide the AI with concrete examples to set the scope and guide its suggestions. This helps focus the AI's output on relevant and productive areas. For instance, if you're brainstorming research methods, offer examples of methods you've used or considered to give the AI a starting point.
3. Set constraints to bound solutions: Consider defining clear project parameters to prevent the AI from generating impractical ideas. This can help keep the brainstorming within feasible limits. Be specific about your research context, available resources, and any ethical considerations to ensure the AI's suggestions are realistic and applicable.
4. Ask targeted questions: Use short, pointed questions to elicit specific responses from the AI. This ensures that each exchange builds on the previous one, incrementally refining ideas. Instead of broad queries, try focused questions that prompt the AI to explore specific aspects of your research problem.
5. Evaluate and redirect: Continuously assess the AI's suggestions, identify any assumptions or impracticalities, and redirect the AI to improve its outputs. Don't hesitate to challenge the AI or ask for clarification – this iterative process often leads to more refined and valuable ideas.

By adhering to these principles, we can create a structured yet flexible framework for our AI-assisted ideation sessions. This approach allows us to harness the AI's knowledge base and rapid processing capabilities while maintaining control over the direction and quality of the brainstorming process.

With the above principles at the fore of our ideation journey, the following steps provide a pathway to navigating towards a desired end-point, for example, generating ideas for research projects and research questions. Here's how you might go about it:

1. Compose initial prompt: Start with a clear, context-setting prompt that introduces your research background and constraints and defines the role of the chatbot (e.g. an expert in a specific disciplinary domain and/or skill).
2. Discuss AI suggestions: Critically review the AI's recommendations, identifying any limitations and probing for more refined ideas.
3. Extract viable possibilities: Narrow down the suggestions through iterative exchanges, focusing on promising directions that balance visionary aims with practical realities.
4. Develop details: Further refine the selected ideas into detailed research proposals, including methods, analysis plans, and anticipated outcomes.

To illustrate how this might play out in practice, consider the case study below, exploring a conversation-style interaction between a researcher and an AI chatbot, designed to illustrate how AI might be used to generate research ideas, focusing on one of my favourite topics: AI on the higher education sector.

Case study: leveraging AI for research project ideation

Dr. X, a qualitative researcher at a business school, sought to explore the implications of AI on the higher education sector. As an experienced scholar, they recognised the potential of AI to transform many aspects of education, from teaching and learning to administration and research. However, given the breadth of the topic, they needed assistance in narrowing down their research focus and generating specific project ideas. To aid in this process, they decided to engage with an AI chatbot.

Here are the steps they took to realise the ideation process:

Step 1: Compose initial prompt

Dr. X crafted a carefully worded prompt to set the context for her interaction and wrote the following prompt:

> I'm a qualitative researcher in a business school and I'm interested in exploring the implications of AI on the higher education sector. I have a background in entrepreneurship and applied AI, and experience conducting interviews and focus groups. I'm looking for innovative research project ideas that help me investigate how AI is transforming higher education, e.g. teaching and learning to administration and research. I want to finish the project within a 12-month timeframe. I have limited research funds to carry out the research. With those considerations in mind, please act in the role of an experienced scholar, capable of ideating novel research projects and providing a range of suggestions for potential research directions. This is really important for my career so please do a good job. Thanks!

Step 2: Discuss AI suggestions

The AI chatbot responded with the following suggestions:[2]

AI: Based on your research interests and constraints, here are some potential research project ideas:

1. Investigating the impact of AI-powered personalised learning systems on student engagement and academic performance. This could involve conducting focus groups with students and interviews with educators to understand their experiences and perceptions.
2. Exploring faculty perceptions and experiences with integrating AI tools into their teaching practices. You could interview faculty members across different disciplines to identify challenges, benefits, and best practices.
3. Examining the ethical implications of using AI for student admissions and recruitment decisions. This could involve

analysing institutional policies and conducting interviews with admissions officers and other stakeholders.

4. Analysing the potential of AI to streamline administrative processes and improve operational efficiency in higher education institutions. You could conduct case studies of institutions that have successfully implemented AI solutions and interview key stakeholders to identify lessons learned.

Dr. X: Thanks. I have some thoughts and questions about your suggestions. For the first idea, won't measuring the impact on academic performance require a longer timeframe than 12 months? Also, for the third idea, it's unlikely that I can get access to admissions data. Do you have any recommendations for navigating that?

AI: You raise valid concerns. Regarding the first idea, you could focus on shorter-term indicators of engagement, such as student participation in class discussions or completion of assignments. This could provide valuable insights within your 12-month timeframe, even if the long-term impact on academic performance is not yet measurable. As for the third idea, you're right that accessing admissions data could be challenging. One alternative approach could be to focus on the perspectives of admissions officers and other stakeholders through interviews, without directly analysing sensitive data. You could explore their decision-making processes, ethical considerations, and views on the potential risks and benefits of using AI in admissions.

Dr. X: Ok, great. Thanks. I'm leaning towards the second and fourth ideas, as they seem to strike a balance between addressing important issues and being feasible. For the second idea, do you think it would be better to focus on faculty in specific disciplines or to take a more general approach?

AI: Focusing on specific disciplines could provide a more in-depth understanding of how AI is being integrated into particular subject areas. For example, you could explore how business school faculty are using AI tools in their teaching of marketing, finance, or operations management. This could yield insights that are especially relevant to your own business school context. Alternatively, taking a general approach across disciplines could help identify common challenges and best practices that transcend subject boundaries. This could be valuable for understanding the broader implications of AI for teaching and learning in higher education. Ultimately, the choice depends on your specific research goals and interests. If you aim to generate insights that are directly applicable to your business school, focusing on specific disciplines might be the way to go. If you're more interested in the general landscape of AI in higher education teaching, a cross-disciplinary approach could be fruitful.

Step 3: Extract viable possibilities

Through further discussion with the AI chatbot, Dr. X refined their research ideas:

Dr. X: Thanks. Given my interest in generating insights relevant to business school contexts, it might be best to focus on how business school faculty are integrating AI into their teaching. I like the suggestion of conducting case studies of institutions that have successfully implemented AI solutions. Please make the approach more manageable given my limited time and budget. Focus on a specific area of administration, such as student services.

AI: Absolutely! Narrowing down the focus to a specific area of administration is a great way to make the project more feasible while still generating valuable insights. Given your interest in the business school context, you could focus on how AI is being used to streamline student services such as academic advising, career counseling, or student engagement initiatives. For example, you could conduct case studies of business schools that have implemented AI-powered chatbots for providing personalized academic guidance to students. This could involve interviewing administrators, advisors, and students to understand the implementation process, perceived benefits and challenges, and lessons learned. Alternatively, you could explore how AI is being used to optimise financial aid processes, such as automating the review of scholarship applications or providing personalized financial aid advice to students. Again, case studies of institutions that have successfully implemented such solutions could yield valuable insights.

Dr. X: Great! I like the idea of focusing on AI-powered chatbots for academic advising in the business school context.

Step 4: Develop details

Dr. X worked with the AI chatbot to flesh out the details of her chosen research project:

Dr. X: Let's focus on "AI-powered chatbots for academic advising in business schools". Please develop a more detailed plan for the study. Maybe a qualitative case study approach. What do you think? What are some specific research questions and methods?

AI: Given your chosen focus, some potential research questions could include:

1. What motivated business schools to implement AI-powered chatbots for academic advising, and what were their goals and expectations?
2. How were the chatbots designed and developed, and what challenges were encountered during the implementation process?
3. How do advisors and students perceive and experience the use of chatbots for academic advising, and what are the perceived benefits and limitations?
4. What lessons can be learned from the experiences of business schools that have successfully implemented AI-powered chatbots for academic advising?

In terms of methods, a qualitative case study approach involving semi-structured interviews with key stakeholders (e.g. administrators, advisors, students) would be well-suited to exploring these questions in depth. You could select a sample of business schools that have implemented AI-powered chatbots for academic advising and conduct interviews with individuals involved in the implementation and use of these technologies.

To analyse the data, you could use a thematic analysis approach, identifying common themes and patterns across the interviews. This could be complemented by a review of relevant documents (e.g. project plans, chatbot design specifications) to provide additional context and triangulate findings.

The ultimate goal would be to generate a rich, nuanced understanding of the experiences and lessons learned from the implementation of AI-powered chatbots for academic advising in business schools. The findings could inform best practices and guidelines for other institutions considering similar initiatives.

Dr. X: Fantastic, thanks! I'll think that over and get back to you.

Case conclusion

If you picked up on the overly polite and conversational style of prompting (see Chapter 7 for an overview of using "please" and "thank you" in prompt writing) and academic background alignment, you probably guessed that the above chatbot conversation was between me and an AI model.

Reflecting on the exchange, it demonstrates the potential of AI as a collaborative partner. Namely, the availability of an AI chatbot to help generate a range of research ideas, respond to specific concerns, and help refine the project focus.

The process highlights the nature of iterative dialogue. Each exchange with the AI built upon the previous one, allowing for a gradual refinement of ideas. This approach mirrors the collaborative brainstorming sessions I might have with colleagues, but with the added benefit of the AI's vast knowledge base, ability to quickly generate and adapt ideas, and 24–7 access – while my colleagues are amazing people, they probably wouldn't appreciate a call to discuss a research project during my vampiric-style work hours. While human collaboration remains invaluable, the AI's tireless availability can be a significant asset, especially for those of us prone to late-night bursts of inspiration.

It's also worth noting that while the AI provided some input to help me work through my thinking, the final research design still requires my professional judgement. The AI's suggestions mostly serve as a springboard for my thinking, rather than a prescription to be followed blindly. This underscores the complementary nature of AI in academic research – it's a powerful tool to augment our capabilities, not replace our expertise.

Lastly, this exercise demonstrated the practical application of the guiding principles for AI-assisted ideation, as discussed earlier in this book. By establishing clear roles, seeding discussions with examples, setting constraints, asking targeted questions, and continuously evaluating and redirecting, you increase your chances of steering the conversation towards a productive outcome.

While the above dialogue with the AI model was somewhat organic, there are several ways that you could bring a more structured approach to the process of brainstorming with AI.

Next, let's explore some more structured techniques for using AI chatbots to generate creative ideas for potential research projects.

Moving beyond "obvious" AI outputs

Back-and-forth conversations with AI chatbots can lead to rapid idea generation – if there's one thing chatbots excel at, it's quickly producing ideas. However, I often find these ideas to be somewhat "obvious". Engaging in this process can leave me questioning whether the chatbot truly helped push the boundaries of my thinking, or if I was just in need of a good old chat and my machine-pals were the only ones available at that late hour to listen to my ramblings.

As discussed in earlier chapters, chatbots can be thought of as prediction machines, making suggestions that could be considered the most probable response. This is great for generalist-style outputs, but for research that might inform a truly innovative study, we're unlikely to want to state the obvious. After all, we'd prefer to avoid a desk rejection accompanied by the dreaded editor response: "This paper is not new and states the obvious". Ouch.

Using long-established creative thinking techniques, such as remote association,[3] and divergent thinking,[4] can help us push beyond the obvious. I first encountered these techniques while studying for a Masters of Entrepreneurship and Innovation. One of my lecturers was particularly enamoured with the work of Edward De Bono, who promoted approaches to free us from the constraints of habitual thought patterns.[5]

While far from being an exhaustive list, consider using the following techniques to brainstorm your next research project:

- Remote association: This technique involves drawing comparisons between seemingly disparate concepts or domains to reveal new insights and possibilities. For example, a researcher studying organisational change could ask an AI chatbot to help identify analogies from nature, such as the process of metamorphosis in butterflies or the adaptive resilience of ecosystems. By exploring these analogies in depth, they may gain fresh perspectives on the drivers, stages, and challenges of organisational transformation.

- Assumption reversal: This approach involves identifying the underlying assumptions or beliefs that shape current thinking about a research topic, and then deliberately challenging or inverting those assumptions. For instance, a researcher investigating the factors that contribute to student success in online learning could ask the AI chatbot to help articulate the prevailing assumptions (e.g. students with strong self-motivation and time management skills are more likely to succeed in online courses). The researcher could then explore the implications of reversing those assumptions (e.g. what if students with weaker self-motivation and time management skills could be equally or even more successful in online learning?). This exercise can open new avenues for research and theory development.
- Divergent thinking: This technique involves generating a wide range of ideas or possibilities without judging or evaluating them in the moment. The goal is to encourage free-flowing, unconstrained thinking that can lead to unexpected connections and insights. Engage in a divergent thinking exercise with the AI chatbot by rapidly brainstorming a list of potential research questions or hypotheses without stopping to assess their feasibility or relevance. Subsequently, review the list and identify the most promising or intriguing ideas for further development.
- Lateral thinking: This approach involves intentionally disrupting linear, logical thought processes to explore new directions and possibilities. One classic lateral thinking technique is the "random entry point" method, where a random word or concept is introduced into the problem-solving process to stimulate new associations and ideas. For instance, a researcher examining the challenges of remote teamwork could ask the AI chatbot to suggest a random object (e.g. "umbrella") and then explore how the features or characteristics of that object might relate to the research topic (e.g. "an umbrella provides shelter and protection from the elements; how might remote teams create a sense of "shelter" or "protection" for their members in a virtual work environment?").

Let's explore some practical examples of how applying creative thinking techniques to the process of ideating research projects might play out in practice.

Scenario: The '5 whys' approach

This technique was popularised through its use at Toyota and involves repeatedly asking 'why' questions.[6] Think of it like a curious child repeatedly asking their parents "But why..." over, and over, and over, again. From a creative thinking perspective, it can be used to move us deeper into understanding the root causes or underlying issues related to our research topics.

Here's an example:

Researcher: I'm interested in studying the impact of AI on job displacement.
AI: One potential angle could be to explore why certain industries or occupations are more vulnerable to AI-driven job displacement.
Researcher: Why are some industries more vulnerable than others?
AI: It could be because some industries involve tasks that are more easily automated or replicated by AI algorithms.
Researcher: Why are some tasks more easily automated?
The conversation continues...

Scenario: Random association

As introduced above, this technique involves introducing random or seemingly unrelated concepts into the conversation to spark new connections and ideas. The researcher can ask the AI chatbot to make associations between the research topic and a randomly chosen word or phrase, leading to unexpected and potentially innovative research directions. For example:

Researcher: I'm studying the role of social media in political polarisation. Let's try a random association. Use the word "underwater".
AI: Interesting! We could explore the concept of "echo chambers" on social media as being similar to underwater caves – isolated, self-reinforcing environments that amplify certain views and limit exposure to diverse perspectives.

Researcher: Great. It makes me think about the role of algorithms in creating these echo chambers, like currents directing the flow of information underwater.
The conversation continues, with the researcher prompting the AI to explore the idea further, in the context of the randomly chosen word or phrase.

Scenario: Combinatorial creativity

This approach goes all the way back to Einstein.[7] It involves combining ideas or elements from different domains to generate novel research questions or hypotheses. In practice, a researcher could ask an AI chatbot to help identify relevant concepts or frameworks from other fields that could be applied to the research topic at hand. Here's an example:

Researcher: I'm interested in studying the factors that contribute to successful startup incubators. What ideas from other domains might be relevant?

AI: One idea from ecology could be the concept of "keystone species" – organisms that play a crucial role in maintaining the structure and function of an ecosystem. In the context of startup incubators, we could explore the role of "keystone mentors" or "keystone investors" who are critical to the success of the incubator ecosystem.

Researcher: Thanks. We could also draw on ideas from developmental psychology, like the concept of "scaffolding" – how incubators provide structured support for startups to grow and develop over time. Please explore this.
The conversation continues...

Incorporating the above ideation techniques into your conversations with AI chatbots can provide a more structured approach to tapping into new sources of creativity and insight. I encourage you to test some of them and see what the chatbot generates.

However, never forget who's in charge!

You should always be "driving the bus", with AI chatbots employed as collaborative sounding boards. And, always maintain an awareness of the limits of today's conversational AI models. While AI chatbots can be skilled sounding boards for early-phase concept exploration, relying wholly on AI ideation forfeits opportunities to cultivate creativity intrinsic to scholarship.

To wrap up this chapter, it's worth emphasising that the creative ideation techniques we've explored can certainly be undertaken *without* AI's assistance.

While prominent AI enthusiasts might recommend *always* inviting AI to the party,[8] and I find myself increasingly doing so, there's undeniable value in occasionally stepping away from our screens.[9] Sometimes, the best course of action to ideate your next research project is to turn off your computer, take a walk, and allow the fresh air to stimulate your creative juices.[10]

With those thoughts in mind, it's time to put the concepts presented in this chapter into practice. To reinforce your understanding and help you develop these skills further, consider completing the activities below before proceeding to the next chapter.

Activity

Use this activity to explore how creative thinking techniques can be combined with AI-assisted ideation to generate innovative research ideas.

Activity: Applying creative thinking techniques

Instructions:

1. Select a research challenge or problem you are currently facing.
2. Choose one of the creative thinking techniques discussed in this chapter.
3. Engage in a dialogue with an AI chatbot, applying the chosen technique to explore new perspectives and ideas related to your research challenge.
4. Analyse the AI's responses and reflect on how the creative thinking technique influenced the ideation process.

Then, consider the following:

- How did the creative thinking technique help you approach the research challenge in a new way?
- What insights or ideas emerged from the AI-assisted ideation process that you might not have considered otherwise?

Reflection and discussion

The following questions aim to help you explore the ideas covered in this chapter. Explore them individually or use them as the basis for group discussion.

1. This chapter suggests that AI-assisted ideation could potentially accelerate the pace of scientific discovery and innovation. However, what potential drawbacks or unintended consequences might arise from this acceleration, and how can they be addressed?
2. How might the integration of AI chatbots into the research ideation process influence the way we value and assess creativity and originality in academic work?
3. Imagine a scenario where a researcher becomes overly reliant on AI-generated ideas and fails to critically evaluate them. What potential risks or pitfalls might arise from this situation, and how might they be mitigated?

Notes

1. Smith, P. G., & Reinertsen, D. G. (1997). *Developing Products in Half the Time: New Rules, New Tools*. John Wiley & Sons.
2. The AI-generated output in this case example was generated using Claude 3.5 Sonnet.
3. Mednick, S. (1962). The associative basis of the creative process. *Psychological Review*, *69*(3), 220–232. https://doi.org/10.1037/h0048850
4. Baer, J. (2014). *Creativity and Divergent Thinking: A Task-Specific Approach*. Psychology Press.

5. De Bono, E. (2009). *Lateral Thinking: A Textbook of Creativity*. Penguin UK.
6. Ohno, T. (2019). *Toyota Production System: Beyond Large-Scale Production*. CRC Press.
7. Rigby, A. (2024, January 14). How to boost your creativity the Einstein way – with combinatory play. *Work Life by Atlassian*. https://www.atlassian.com/blog/productivity/combinatory-play-boost-creativity
8. Mollick, E. (2024). *Co-Intelligence: Living and Working with AI*. Random House.
9. Newport, C. (2019). *Digital Minimalism: Living Better with Less Technology*. Penguin UK.
10. Yu, C., & Hsieh, H. (2020). Beyond restorative benefits: Evaluating the effect of forest therapy on creativity. *Urban Forestry & Urban Greening, 51*, 126670. https://doi.org/10.1016/j.ufug.2020.126670

AI-powered literature search

Introduction

As a fellow researcher, you're likely no stranger to the challenges of information overload. With the exponential growth of scholarly publications, data, and online resources, the process of finding relevant information to inform your literature review can feel like searching for the proverbial needle in a haystack.[1] Rather than helping to develop knowledge, the rising number of papers scholars need to navigate to stay abreast of their research domain has been found to be impeding the rise of scholarship.[2]

For most of my academic career, the process for finding academic papers has remained relatively the same, relying on keyword-based search methods to navigate available literature.

This approach would see me spending hours scrolling through search results, which often lacked relevance to meeting my search intent. Fortunately, this situation is changing with the arrival of AI-powered literature search tools.[3]

In this chapter, we'll explore how AI is transforming literature search, focusing on the game-changing potential of "semantic search" – a method that aims to understand the meaning and context of your query, rather than just matching keywords. We'll also examine the mechanisms behind semantic search tools, discuss strategies for their effective use, and consider both the opportunities and challenges they present for academic research.

Let's begin by understanding some of the limitations of traditional search methods and how semantic search is moving towards addressing these challenges.

DOI: 10.4324/9781032665276-9

From keywords to concepts

Traditional keyword-based search methods have been the backbone of the academic literature discovery process for decades. Popular search tools, like Google Scholar.[4] have primarily operated by matching the words in your search query with those found in the titles, abstracts, and full text of academic papers. While the exact algorithms these systems use are proprietary, the core principle is thought to revolve around word matching. This approach has served researchers well, providing a straightforward way to find relevant literature. However, it comes with several notable limitations that can affect the comprehensiveness and relevance of our search efforts.

The first is the potential lack of context. When search results are based on keywords, the system may struggle to understand the meaning behind your words. For example, the word "bank" might return a search result about financial institutions or riverbanks indiscriminately. Based only on the keyword "bank", it's hard to know which of those options constitutes a well-matched result. Additionally, synonyms and polysemy also play a role in limiting the value of keyword-based search results – the search may miss relevant papers that use synonyms or conversely, results might include irrelevant results due to words having multiple meanings.

There is also the issue of the limitations of a researcher's vocabulary. The effectiveness of keyword searches can depend heavily on the researcher's ability to choose the right terms in their search query, which can be particularly challenging in interdisciplinary studies where terminology may vary across fields, or for non-native English speakers who may not be familiar with all relevant terms of their nuances when searching among a sea of English language papers.[5]

Semantic search, powered by AI, aims to address these limitations by focusing on the meaning and context of search queries, rather than just matching words.

Here's how semantic search differs from traditional methods:

1. Understanding context: Semantic search algorithms analyse the relationships between words and concepts, allowing them to "understand" the intent behind a search query.

2. Handling language variations: These systems can recognise synonyms, related terms, and even concepts that are semantically related but lexically different.
3. Concept-based matching: Instead of simply matching words, semantic search works by matching concepts, allowing it to find relevant papers even when different terminology is used.
4. Natural language processing: Many semantic search tools can handle natural language queries, making the search process more intuitive and user-friendly. This allows the researcher to "talk" to AI literature search tools in a similar manner in which you'd ask a research assistant to locate papers for you on a certain topic.

To illustrate the difference between traditional keyword search and semantic search, consider a researcher looking for papers on the effect of excessive coffee consumption on academic performance. A traditional keyword search might use terms like "coffee", "caffeine", "academic performance", and "students". This approach could miss papers that use terms like "stimulants" instead of "coffee", or "cognitive function" instead of "academic performance". By comparison, a semantic search could understand the concepts behind the query. It might include papers that discuss "psychoactive substances" and their impact on "cognitive abilities in educational settings", even if they don't use the exact terms in the original query. It could also recognise related concepts like "sleep deprivation", "study habits", or "exam stress", broadening the scope of relevant results to include factors that might interact with coffee consumption in affecting academic performance.

Let's explore how this process works from a slightly more technical perspective.

'Under the hood' of semantic search

The magic of semantic search lies in its ability to interpret human language in a way that mimics human comprehension. It's achieved through a combination of advanced AI technologies, primarily natural language processing (NLP) and machine learning (ML), which were touched on in Chapter 5. Let's take a closer look at each:

- NLP is a branch of AI that focuses on the interaction between computers and human language. In the context of semantic search, NLP algorithms are used to analyse the meaning of both the search query and the academic texts being returned by the AI tool. Key techniques involved in NLP include tokenisation (i.e. breaking text into smaller units called tokens); syntactic parsing (i.e. analysing the grammatical structure of sentences); and semantic analysis (i.e. understanding the meaning and relationships between words and phrases).
- ML models, which are typically trained on vast corpora of data (including academic literature) learn the relationships between words, phrases, and concepts, drawing on word embedding techniques, and neural networks – deep learning models that capture the nature of complex relationships in language.

To illustrate how they work together, imagine you type the following query into an AI-powered literature search tool: "The impact of climate change on marine ecosystems".

A semantic search process might play out as follows:

1. NLP algorithms would first analyse your query, identifying key concepts like "climate change" and "marine ecosystems".
2. The system would use machine learning models to identify related concepts, such as "global warming", "coral bleaching", or "sea level rise".
3. It might then consult a knowledge graph (i.e. a structured representation of relationships) to understand the relationships between these concepts and identify relevant sub-topics or related fields of study.
4. The search would then be expanded to include these related terms and concepts.
5. The system would subsequently search through its database of academic literature, using NLP to analyse the content of papers and identify those that discuss relevant concepts, even if you didn't use those exact words in your original query.
6. Finally, machine learning algorithms would rank the results based on their relevance to the original query and the expanded concepts.

This process allows for a comprehensive and nuanced set of search results.

While you don't need to know exactly what's going on "under the hood" of AI to become an AI-powered scholar, having an awareness of the background processes can help you make more informed decisions about when to use an AI tool for literature searches and when to rely on traditional methods. In my own practice, I've incorporated AI search tools into my research workflows alongside traditional search tools, which might lead you to think that I've added to my workload rather than reducing it. Perhaps. But, I've found significant benefits in including AI literature search into the mix. The primary advantage is that I often discover papers I wouldn't have found through traditional methods alone. And secondly, if I'm starting out on a new research project, and don't yet know what keywords might return the best results, I find turning to semantic-based tools more beneficial in helping me to initially gather literature that's attuned to helping me explore the topic. Overall, using a combination of AI and traditional tools generally provides a more comprehensive view of the available literature, often revealing unexpected connections or less obvious but highly relevant studies.

Next, we'll explore practical strategies for leveraging these AI-powered tools in practice.

Conducting AI-powered literature search

Now that you have a basic understanding of how AI-powered semantic search works, let's explore how to integrate semantic search tools into your research workflows.

Here are some strategies and approaches:

1. If you're new to a topic, try starting broad, then refine: Begin with a broad search query that captures the main concepts of your research topic. AI-powered tools can help you identify related concepts and subtopics you might not have considered. As you review the results, you can then refine your search based on the most relevant themes that emerge. The process is highly exploratory and can lead to some interesting results.
2. Use natural language queries: Remember, when interacting with chatbots, it's best to phrase your interactions as if you were speaking

to a human. Semantic search tools are typically designed to understand natural language – phrase your queries accordingly. Instead of trying to craft the perfect combination of keywords, try phrasing your search as a question or a statement. For example, you might ask: "What are the effects of mindfulness meditation on overworked academics?"

3. Combine the AI's insights with your "human" expertise: While AI can provide valuable suggestions and connections, you should remain in the driver's seat. You are (or are hopefully on the path to becoming) a subject knowledge expert. Drawing on this expertise is important. Use the AI's suggestions as a starting point, but always apply your critical thinking skills to evaluate the relevance and quality of the suggested literature.
4. Iterative searching: Use the insights gained from initial searches to refine and expand your search strategy. AI-powered tools can help you identify new keywords, related concepts, or influential papers that you can use to guide further searches. This can lead to a divergent creative thinking process whereby your initial topic is expanded to bring in new perspectives during the ideation phase.
5. Cross-disciplinary exploration: Semantic search is particularly powerful for identifying relevant research from adjacent fields. Consider leveraging this capability to explore how your research topic might intersect with other disciplines.
6. Validate and verify: Remember that while AI tools are powerful, they're not infallible. Credible AI search tools tend to hyperlink to the sources they are citing. It goes without saying that before you cite a paper in your research you should ensure that the paper actually exists and also read it (!!).

Challenges and limitations of AI-powered literature search

While AI-powered semantic search offers tremendous benefits for academic research, it's important to be aware of its limitations and potential challenges.

Here are some things to consider, alongside some of the potential issues and strategies for responsible AI use, raised earlier in Chapter 7:

1. Bias in training data: AI models are trained on existing academic literature, which may contain historical biases. This could lead to the perpetuation of these biases in search results. For example, research from certain countries or in certain languages might be underrepresented.
2. Overreliance on AI suggestions: There's a risk of becoming overly dependent on AI-generated suggestions, potentially missing important papers that the AI system fails to identify. In the scope of AI's current capabilities, I would never rely on just one AI tool as a single source of truth for finding academic literature. Consider using AI tools alongside more traditional search options.
3. Lack of transparency: The complex algorithms behind semantic search can sometimes act as a "black box",[6] making it difficult to understand why certain results are presented. In effect, there is little "explainability" for the results you received. This lack of transparency can be problematic in academic research, where the ability to justify and explain one's literature search method may be crucial (e.g. when conducting a systematic literature review).
4. Limited coverage: Depending on the tool you use to conduct your semantic search enquiries, the database of academic literature it searches might not be comprehensive. Some important papers, especially from niche fields or non-mainstream publications, might be missed.
5. Difficulty with cutting-edge research: AI models are trained on existing literature and may struggle to accurately categorise or connect very recent or cutting-edge research that uses new terminology or concepts. Be mindful of this when interpreting the search results.
6. Over-smoothing of language differences: While the ability to find conceptually related papers regardless of specific terminology is generally beneficial, it might sometimes obscure important nuances in how different researchers or traditions describe similar concepts.

In order to address these challenges, consider the following guiding principles:

1. Maintain critical awareness: Always approach AI-generated results with a critical mindset. Be aware of potential biases and limitations.
2. Combine methods: Use AI-powered tools in conjunction with traditional search methods and human expertise. Cross-reference results from multiple sources.
3. Continuous learning: Stay informed about the latest developments in AI-powered research tools. Understand how they work and what their limitations are.
4. Advocate for transparency: Support and use tools that provide transparency about their algorithms and data sources. You can find these in the AI tool provider's terms and conditions documents, which should be available for any credible AI tool.
5. Supplement with manual searches: Current-day AI is useful, but it does not currently represent the panacea of perfection, and it's often necessary to supplement AI-powered searches with traditional search approaches.

By being aware of these challenges and actively working to address them, you will be better placed to leverage AI in your literature search process while also maintaining the integrity and rigour of your academic work.

To wrap up this chapter, remember that AI-powered literature search, particularly semantic search, represents a significant leap forward in our ability to navigate the seemingly never-ending body of knowledge. By understanding the meaning and context behind our queries, these tools offer an intuitive and comprehensive approach to discovering relevant research to inform our literature reviews.

As AI continues to evolve, we can expect even more sophisticated tools to emerge. It's for this reason that I haven't named specific tools in this chapter, but I promise to include a list of my favourites in the accompanying online companion to this book.[7]

To conclude, I encourage you to approach AI-powered literature search with both enthusiasm and critical awareness. Embrace its potential to enhance your research, but always apply your human judgement and expertise.

Reflection and discussion

To deepen your understanding of AI-powered literature search and its implications for academic research, consider the following questions:

1. How might the widespread adoption of AI-powered semantic search change the way we approach conducting literature reviews? What skills might become more or less important for researchers?
2. Consider a recent literature search you conducted. How might the process and outcomes have been different if you had used an AI-powered semantic search tool? What additional insights might you have gained, and what potential pitfalls might you have encountered?
3. What ethical considerations should guide the development and use of AI in academic literature search? How can we ensure that the use of AI tools promotes equity and diversity in research rather than reinforcing existing biases?

Notes

1. Hesse, C., Sartori, M., & Schmitt, S. (2021). Informetric analysis of scientific literature on semantic search. *Future Internet, 13*(6), 151.
2. Chu, J. S. G., & Evans, J. A. (2021). Slowed canonical progress in large fields of science. *Proceedings of the National Academy of Sciences of the United States of America, 118*(41), 1–2. https://doi.org/10.1073/pnas.2021636118
3. For information on available AI-powered literature search tools, visit broneager.com/aischolar
4. https://scholar.google.com
5. Toledo, E. G. (2024, March 7). English dominates scientific research – here's how we can fix it, and why it matters. *The Conversation*. https://theconversation.com/english-dominates-scientific-research-heres-how-we-can-fix-it-and-why-it-matters-226198?

6. Hassija, V., Chamola, V., Mahapatra, A., Singal, A., Goel, D., Huang, K., Scardapane, S., Spinelli, I., Mahmud, M., & Hussain, A. (2023). Interpreting black-box models: A review on explainable artificial intelligence. *Cognitive Computation*, *16*(1), 45–74. https://doi.org/10.1007/s12559-023-10179-8
7. www.broneager.com/aischolar

10 Writing & editing with AI

Introduction

For many academic writers, me included, there are few tasks more daunting than creating a new document on your computer and knowing that it needs to be filled with words. That blinking cursor, ostensibly patient, waiting for brilliance to flow from fingertips to keyboard, can feel less like an invitation and more like an accusation.

"Well?" it seems to taunt, "Aren't you supposed to be writing something brilliant?"

Fortunately, there's a strategy to break this stalemate: getting some words – any words – on the page. I know that's precisely the hurdle you're trying to overcome, but bear with me as I share how we can call upon AI chatbots to lend a hand (or more accurately, a helping algorithm).

Now, I anticipate some readers thinking, "Isn't using AI for academic writing cheating?" It's a valid concern, one hotly debated since ChatGPT's public launch.[1] As such, it's worth clarifying that its generally not ok to pass off large slaps of AI-generated content as your original work. However, much like brainstorming with a colleague or getting feedback from your supervisor, AI can serve as a thought-provoking collaborator and is increasingly skilled at assisting in translating our often-times rambling thoughts into well-structured text; generating outlines for further development; crafting and refining our academic writing; and as an editorial assistant.

Let's begin by introducing a technique I call "blah writing"'.

DOI: 10.4324/9781032665276-10

Getting your thoughts on the page

As academic writers, we can find ourselves trapped in a paradox of perfectionism. Our minds are alive with ideas, theories, and half-formed arguments, yet the pressure to articulate these thoughts eloquently can leave us paralysed before a blank page. This is where the concept of "Blah writing" comes in.

The term "blah" is often used colloquially in English to represent meaningless or nonsensical talk. You might hear someone say "blah blah blah" to mimic the sound of ongoing, unimportant chatter. Here, I've chosen to reclaim the term for productive purposes, adopting it to title a strategic approach to getting your thoughts out of your head and onto the page.

Blah writing is essentially a digital version of stream of consciousness journaling.[2] It involves typing out your thoughts, ideas, and even your anxieties about your writing task in a rapid, unfiltered manner to an AI chatbot. The goal isn't to produce polished prose, but rather to externalise the whirlwind of thoughts that may be stuck in your head and hindering the writing process.

This approach can be particularly helpful for anyone who feels intimidated by the pressure to produce "perfect" writing from the outset. Blah writing gives you permission to be messy, imperfect, and exploratory.

The following is an example workflow for achieving blah writing alongside an AI chatbot:

1. Set the stage: Begin by assigning your AI chatbot a role, as you learnt about in Chapter 4. You might cast it as a patient, non-judgemental writing coach or a knowledgeable colleague in your field. This helps create a supportive environment for your unfiltered thoughts.
2. Brain dump: Start typing whatever comes to mind about your topic, stream of consciousness style. Don't worry about grammar, structure, or even coherence at this stage. The aim is to get your thoughts out of your head and onto the screen. Let your ideas flow freely, no matter how disjointed or rambling they may seem.
3. Seek synthesis: Once you've externalised your thoughts, use your prompt-writing skills from Chapter 6 to ask the AI to help synthesise your ideas. Request it to clarify your thoughts and translate the mess you've dumped into it into a coherent narrative.

4. Reflect and iterate: Review the AI's suggestions critically. Use them as a catalyst for your own critical thinking and further writing. Consider whether the synthesis accurately reflects your thoughts, if important points were overlooked, and how you might expand on these themes.

An example of how this might play out in practice is as follows:

1. Set the stage: "Please act as a supportive writing coach specialising in educational technology. I need help organising my thoughts on AI implementation in higher education".
2. Brain dump: "What am I doing writing stresses me trying this brain dump of thoughts thesis needs to get written so here goes. Want to talk about adaptive learning AI systems in universities great potential to personalise the student experience by tracking progress and suggesting resources tailored to individual needs but there are huge implementation challenges to consider especially around data privacy and ethical issues like bias in algorithms that could unintentionally disadvantage certain groups we need to think carefully about how lecturers fit into this new paradigm as they might become more like facilitators guiding students through AI-enhanced learning journeys which sounds interesting but could be threatening to some staff members who'll need training and upskilling in AI literacy and effective integration of these systems into the curriculum it's not just a plug and play solution and might require redesigning entire courses which is exciting but daunting and time-consuming with significant resource implications to consider but the potential benefits are substantial like students getting immediate feedback 24/7 which could increase engagement and improve retention rates by helping identify struggling students earlier for timely interventions though we need to balance this with ethical considerations about how much monitoring is too much and ensure accessibility for students with disabilities it's a complex topic with lots to consider but definitely worth exploring further as it could revolutionise higher education".
3. Seek synthesis: "Can you please rephrase this jumbled paragraph into a more coherent narrative? I'm trying to articulate my thoughts on adaptive learning AI systems in higher education more clearly".

AI-generated response:[3] "Certainly. Here's a more coherent narrative based on your thoughts:

Adaptive learning AI systems offer significant potential for personalising the student experience in higher education. These systems can track individual progress and suggest tailored resources, potentially leading to increased engagement, improved retention rates, and earlier identification of struggling students for timely interventions.

However, the implementation of such systems presents considerable challenges. Primary concerns include data privacy and ethical issues, particularly the risk of algorithmic bias that could inadvertently disadvantage certain student groups.

Moreover, the integration of AI systems may necessitate a fundamental shift in teaching roles, with lecturers potentially evolving into facilitators who guide students through AI-enhanced learning journeys. This transition is not without its hurdles. It requires substantial investment in staff training, focusing on AI literacy and the effective integration of these systems into the curriculum. The process may involve redesigning entire courses, which, while potentially exciting, is also daunting, time-consuming, and resource-intensive.

Furthermore, ethical considerations must be carefully balanced. While continuous monitoring can provide valuable insights, it's crucial to establish appropriate boundaries to protect student privacy.

Additionally, ensuring accessibility for students with disabilities must be a priority in the development and implementation of these AI systems.

In conclusion, while adaptive learning AI systems present complex challenges, their potential to revolutionise higher education makes them a topic worthy of further exploration and careful consideration".

4. Reflect and iterate: "This is a great start, thanks..."

   The conversation would continue, with the academic reflecting on the AI's suggestions, asking for further clarification or expansion as needed, and being in a position to start adding to the text and getting more words on the page.

As you can see from the worked example above, "blah writing" can transform a chaotic stream of thoughts into a "draft zero", comprising a structured, coherent narrative. It can help you to overcome the initial hurdle of writer's block but also provide you with a foundation for further development of your ideas. Remember that the goal is not necessarily the production of a finished product, but to kickstart your writing process and generate a base from which to build.

Generating outlines

Another strategy for overcoming writing roadblocks with AI chatbots is to employ their capabilities to create a comprehensive outline for your upcoming publication. By generating headings and subheadings, AI can help create a "paint by numbers" scenario, eliminating the guesswork about what to write next. This method draws on the approach of Professor Rowena Murray,[4] who visited my university during my PhD candidature and changed the way I approached future writing tasks. During her session, and as is well documented in her many books, she recommended creating highly prescriptive outlines, including specifying word counts for each section.

These detailed outlines allow you to approach your writing flexibly, enabling you to work on any section at any time, simply by filling in the required number of words. Essentially, they provide you with a framework for structuring your thoughts and can take away some of the stress of the intimidating expanse of white space, replaced by a clear action plan which you can dip in and out of as time permits.

To create an outline with the help of AI, I recommend beginning by assigning your AI assistant a role.

An example role prompt could look something like this:

> Please assume the role of a senior research assistant with expertise in [Insert topic, e.g., educational technology and AI implementation in higher education]. You have a background in qualitative research and twenty years of experience writing academic papers for high-quality journals. Communicate in a professional yet approachable tone, and don't hesitate to ask for clarification if needed.

You might also provide an exemplar outline, based on an existing paper. This approach is particularly beneficial when you aim to emulate a specific structure or style common in your field of study. By doing so, you're essentially giving the AI a template to work from, ensuring that your outline aligns with established conventions in your discipline. But, before uploading anything, ensure you have the necessary permissions. Most leading AI models are capable of extracting the outline from an uploaded document, so there's no need for you to go through the document and type it out.

For instance, you might prompt:

> I've uploaded a paper titled [Paper Title] that follows the structure I'd like to emulate. Please analyse this paper's structure, focusing on its headings and subheadings. Then, using this structure as a guide, create an outline for a 5,000-word paper on [Your Topic]. Adapt the headings and subheadings to fit my topic while maintaining a similar overall structure. For each section, please suggest an approximate word count.

If you don't have an exemplar outline/paper, you might use a prompt like this:

> Please create a detailed outline for a 5,000-word academic paper on [Your topic]. The paper should follow a standard research article structure including an introduction, literature review, methodology, results, discussion, and conclusion. Please provide main headings and subheadings and suggest an approximate word count for each section. The outline should be suitable for a qualitative research paper to be submitted to a peer-reviewed journal in [Your field]. Thanks!

For example, if your topic was "The Impact of AI on Higher Education Teaching Practices", your prompt might look like this:

> Please create a detailed outline for a 5,000-word academic paper on 'The Impact of AI on Higher Education Teaching Practices'. The paper should follow a standard research article structure including an introduction, literature review, methodology, results, discussion, and conclusion. Please provide main headings and subheadings and suggest an approximate word

> count for each section. The outline should be suitable for a qualitative research paper to be submitted to a peer-reviewed journal in educational technology. Thanks.

Remember, while AI can provide a valuable starting point, the final structure should always be refined based on your unique insights, research findings, and the specific requirements of your academic project.

Expanding text

There are often times when we find ourselves needing to elaborate on our ideas or deepen the level of description to justify our arguments. In other words: we find ourselves in need of more words so that we can satisfy required wordcounts. AI tools can be used for this task by assisting us in rephrasing our already-written text, suggesting additional points, and by offering ways we could expand our writing to achieve greater depth and clarity.

If you're thinking of using AI for this task, it's important to exhibit some caution.

As was discussed in Chapter 7, AI-generated content contains many limitations (e.g. hallucinations) and should always be critically evaluated and refined through your own expertise and judgement. Therefore, while, in theory, people are presumed innocent until proven guilty in courtrooms, the opposite mindset is wise to apply to AI-generated content, especially when that content is contributing to the creation of academic publications! I always take a "guilty until proven innocent" approach when encountering AI-generated text – every AI suggestion is treated with a healthy dose of scepticism, and only "acquitted" after thorough verification.

With this firmly front of mind, let's explore how you might use AI chatbots to expand a sample of your academic writing:

To use an AI chatbot for expanding text:

1. Identify the section to expand: Highlight the specific paragraph or passage that you want to develop further.
2. Provide a clear prompt: Give the AI chatbot a specific instruction for expansion, such as "Please provide more detailed explanations of the

key concepts in this paragraph", "Suggest ways to elaborate on the evidence presented here to strengthen the argument", or simply use a prompt such as "Please expand this text".

3. Review and refine: Read through the AI's suggestions and integrate the most relevant and useful expansions. Be sure to maintain your own voice and style and ensure that any added material enhances rather than detracts from your overall argument.

If you try this approach, I urge you to think of yourself as both a collaborator and a gatekeeper – working with the AI to generate ideas, but carefully filtering and refining its output. Remember, the goal is not just to increase your word count, but also to enhance the depth, clarity, and overall quality of your work.

Contracting text

At the start of a writing project our goal tends to be focused on generating *more* words. However, there will likely come a time when you also need to cut them back. For example, when you receive a dreaded "desk reject" and find out that the next journal on your list of potential homes for your paper has a significantly lower maximum word count. AI chatbots can help speed up the process by suggesting ways to eliminate redundancies, trim extraneous details, and articulate your core message.

Here's one way you might get the job done:

1. Select the text you want to shorten: First, highlight the paragraph or passage you're focusing on. Then, save it temporarily by copying it. This allows you to use it again right away without having to retype it.
2. Provide a clear prompt: Give the AI chatbot a specific instruction for contraction, such as "Please suggest ways to eliminate unnecessary details and make this passage more concise", or "Identify any redundant or repetitive phrases that could be removed from this paragraph".
3. Review and refine: Read through the AI's suggestions and integrate the most relevant and useful contractions into your text. Be mindful not to remove any essential information or nuance and ensure that your condensed version still effectively communicates your key points.

To demonstrate how this process works in practice, let's look at an example. The following output was generated using Claude, an AI chatbot running its 3.5 Sonnet model. Claude generated a result (reproduced below) after being provided with the following sample text and prompt:

> Sample text: The researchers conducted in-depth, semi-structured interviews with 15 university lecturers who had implemented AI-powered adaptive learning systems in their courses. The interviews, lasting between 60 and 90 minutes each, were conducted via video conferencing software due to COVID-19 restrictions. The interview questions focused on the lecturers' experiences with the AI systems, their perceptions of the impact on student learning, and the challenges they faced during implementation. All interviews were audio-recorded with participant consent and subsequently transcribed verbatim. The researchers then employed a thematic analysis approach, following Braun and Clarke's six-step process, to identify key themes and patterns in the data. This involved multiple rounds of coding and theme refinement, with regular team meetings to discuss and validate the emerging findings.
>
> Prompt: "Please suggest ways to make this passage more concise by removing unnecessary details and streamlining the description of the qualitative research process, while maintaining the essential methodological information".
>
> Contracted text: "Semi-structured interviews were conducted with 15 university lecturers who had implemented AI-powered adaptive learning systems. Interviews, conducted virtually, explored lecturers' experiences, perceived impacts on student learning, and implementation challenges. Using Braun and Clarke's thematic analysis approach, researchers identified key themes through iterative coding and team validation".

As with all aspects of AI-assisted writing, it's important to approach these suggestions with a critical eye and with a commitment to maintaining your own authorial voice and intent. It's best to consider the chatbot's recommendations as a starting point for refinement, ensuring that you always make the final decisions about what to include and what to cut.

Editing with AI

Between teaching responsibilities, conducting research, analysing data, and juggling university admin, having the headspace to conduct a thorough edit of your work can be a challenge. For those fortunate enough to have access to a professional editor, willing colleague, caring supervisor, or generous friend, the benefit of having a skilled human look over your work can't be overstated. Unfortunately, there are many barriers to acquiring editorial assistance. And while AI tools are currently far from perfect compared to a professional editor, they do offer some benefits worth considering, including:

1. Round-the-clock availability: AI chatbots don't keep office hours. They're ready to assist you whenever you need.
2. Instant feedback: With an AI chatbot, you don't have to wait days or weeks for feedback on your writing. Suggestions are provided in real time, allowing you to iterate and improve your work according to your schedule.
3. Cost-effective solution: Human editors can cost thousands of dollars, especially when tasked with editing lengthy academic documents. AI chatbots offer a relatively affordable alternative, at least in terms of your out-of-pocket expenses.[5]
4. A "safe space": Sometimes we're hesitant to share our writing with others for fear of judgement. Chatbots can offer a sounding board without that fear attached. Additionally, they are typically trained to offer supportive advice, unless, of course, you decide to prompt your chatbot to "provide critiques in the style of a grumpy academic at a conference, poised to unleash scathing comments during the Q&A".

To use an AI chatbot in the editing process, you will (obviously) need some text that requires editing. It could be as small as a sentence, or as large as thesis. When you've got some words to work with, here's an example workflow for completing the process:

1. Choose your AI platform: For longer edits, select a platform that has document upload capabilities. This feature allows you to input larger

portions of text or entire documents for analysis. Importantly – ensure that the platform you choose complies with your institution's data protection and privacy policies.

2. Prepare your document: Before uploading, review your document to ensure it doesn't contain any sensitive or confidential information.
3. Upload the document: Follow the platform's instructions for uploading your document. This usually involves selecting the file from your computer (typically by clicking on a paperclip icon), or cloud storage provider, or copying and pasting your text into a designated area.
4. Prompt the chatbot: This is where your skills in crafting effective prompts (if you need a refresh, see Chapter 6) come into play. Be specific about what kind of editing assistance you need. For example: "Please review this text for clarity and coherence. Suggest improvements in sentence structure, identify any awkward phrasing, and highlight areas where the argument could be strengthened. Pay particular attention to the flow between paragraphs and the use of academic language".
5. Review the analysis: Carefully read through the AI's suggestions. While AI can provide valuable insights, it's not infallible.

Lastly, always use your critical thinking skills to evaluate each suggestion, considering:

- Does the suggested change improve clarity or flow?
- Does it maintain your intended meaning?
- Is it consistent with your voice and style?

As you become more comfortable with AI-assisted editing, you might find it particularly useful for tasks such as:

- Checking for consistency in terminology and style
- Identifying overused words or phrases
- Suggesting more precise vocabulary
- Highlighting areas where citations might be needed
- Improving the overall structure and flow of your argument

It's important to recognise that what's been covered in this chapter, and the book more broadly, is just the tip of the iceberg when it comes to leveraging AI in academic tasks.

If you're enthusiastic to explore additional AI applications, you'll find the final chapter of this book to be an invaluable resource. It provides access to online materials, including practical use cases, allowing you to continue your journey into AI-powered scholarship.

That's a wrap!

It was tempting to conclude this book with a playful snippet of AI-generated text. Perhaps by using a prompt such as: "Please craft a three-line poem, that expresses to my family and friends that, finally, the book has been written, and I'll soon be returning to pre-ChatGPT patterns of social interaction after having a day off to celebrate".

But just as non-disclosed AI-generated content continues to be judged as a misrepresentation of human effort, so too would that poem's sentiments misrepresent any intention of dialling down my enthusiasm for building AI skills and sharing them widely. I long jumped down the rabbit hole of AI, and, like many other AI enthusiasts who attached themselves to the AI rocket ship, I continue to thrive on its energy.

The pace of advancement, including the almost daily updates about new features, apps, business cases, etc. provides more dopamine hits than a bottle of Vyvanse.[6] AI has significantly enhanced my life, and through sharing some of what I've learnt so far, I hope to have nudged you towards unlocking similar benefits.

Yet, many across the sector are understandably panicked by AI, viewing it as the end of academic scholarship and the death of academic writing.

Which is why I'd like to ask you a small favour.

Remember when we metaphorically unwrapped the gift of AI in Chapter 1? Now that you've journeyed through this book, you've hopefully not only unwrapped that gift but have begun to feel comfortable using it. This gift is not a zero-sum game. I believe lifting others up on their AI journey will help lift academia more broadly, and thus help us to retain integrity and relevance (and the chances of ongoing employment!) in a sector that's facing massive disruption. I encourage you to become an AI literacy ambassador in your academic community. Share your newfound skills and insights with colleagues and students. Organise workshops, initiate discussions, or simply offer a helping hand to those still grappling with the blinking cursor on a blank page.

Thank you for coming along on the journey through this book. If you now feel a little more comfortable using AI, are a more informed user, or just got some enjoyment from my often-times self-indulgent narrative tangents, I've achieved what I set out to do. If you found value in these pages, I would be very grateful if you could do the proverbial "like and subscribe" on social media to help promote the book online.

Lastly, I urge you to be mindful that the AI revolution in academia isn't just about technology – it's about reimagining the very essence of higher education. But that's a topic for a whole other book!

Notes

1. Jensen, L. X., Buhl, A., Sharma, A., & Bearman, M. (2024). Generative AI and higher education: a review of claims from the first months of ChatGPT. *Higher Education*, 1–17. https://doi.org/10.1007/s10734-024-01265-3
2. Cameron, J. (2020). *The Artist's Way: A Spiritual Path to Higher Creativity*. Souvenir Press.
3. The provided response was generated by Claude.ai, using Claude 3.5 Sonnet.
4. To learn more about Professor Rowena Murray, visit https://www.anchorage-education.co.uk/about-me/
5. For insights into AI's costs, including environmental impacts, refer to: Crawford, K. (2021). *The Atlas of AI: Power, Politics, and the Planetary Costs of Artificial Intelligence*. Yale University Press.
6. Prescription medication used to treat Attention Deficit Hyperactivity Disorder (ADHD).

Bonus chapter

If this book had included mentions of the "best AI tools for the job", they would likely be outdated before the ink dried on the page.

Providing this information via an online companion resource allows it to be as fresh as your morning coffee, updated as new tools emerge and others become obsolete.

Unlock bonus material by visiting: www.broneager.com/aischolar

DOI: 10.4324/9781032665276-11

Glossary

As you work through the chapters in this book, you'll likely encounter some unfamiliar terms. This glossary is designed to be your handy companion for navigating common AI terminology. It's not an exhaustive encyclopaedia of AI jargon but rather a friendly guidebook. Here, you'll find clear and concise explanations of key concepts, essential for building your AI literacy skills.

A

Accuracy (in machine learning) A metric used to evaluate the performance of a machine learning (ML) model, measuring the proportion of correct predictions among the total number of cases examined.

AGI (Artificial General Intelligence) A hypothetical form of AI that would have the ability to understand, learn, and apply intelligence in a way that matches or surpasses human cognitive abilities across a wide range of tasks. Unlike narrow AI, which is designed for specific tasks, AGI would be capable of generalising its knowledge and skills to new situations.

AI-assisted (AI-augmented) This term describes the use of artificial intelligence to enhance human capabilities in various tasks. The primary goal is to increase efficiency, accuracy, and productivity, allowing academics to focus on more innovative and strategic elements of their work. AI-assisted tools act as digital collaborators, augmenting rather than replacing human expertise.

AI-generated (outputs) Content or outputs predominantly created by artificial intelligence systems. Examples include text, images, music, videos, and other data forms. These are often crafted using sophisticated AI techniques such as deep learning and natural language processing. AI systems analyse vast datasets to produce innovative content that showcases human-like creativity or analytical capabilities. The quality and complexity of AI-generated content hinge on various factors, including the algorithms and training data used.

AI literacy The understanding and skill set required to effectively interact with, manage, or leverage artificial intelligence technologies. This encompasses a basic knowledge of what AI is, how it works, and its potential applications. AI literacy goes beyond technical skills, embracing an awareness of ethical considerations, biases in AI, and the impact of AI on various sectors such as employment, privacy, and security.

AI tools Software applications or platforms that incorporate artificial intelligence to perform or improve tasks. AI tools are increasingly being integrated into academic workflows to enhance research and writing processes.

AI winter/AI summer In the history of artificial intelligence research, an "AI winter" refers to a period where progress stagnated, leading to reduced interest and funding. Conversely, an "AI summer" describes a time of accelerated progress, sparking renewed interest and investment in the field.

Algorithm A set of step-by-step instructions or rules designed to perform a specific task or solve a particular problem. In computing, algorithms are used to manipulate, process, and analyse data, forming the basis of computer programs. The efficiency and effectiveness of an algorithm are crucial, as they directly impact the performance and capabilities of a software application or system.

Alignment The consistency of an AI system's actions and decisions with human values and intentions. This involves designing AI models that understand and adhere to ethical guidelines, societal norms, and the specific objectives set by their human developers or users. Alignment is a critical concern in AI safety and ethics, particularly as AI systems become more capable.

Anthropic An artificial intelligence research and safety company founded by former employees of OpenAI (the company behind

ChatGPT). Anthropic focuses on developing large-scale AI models while emphasising AI safety and ethical considerations. Their popularly used chatbot, Claude, is available at www.claude.ai.

API (Application Programming Interface) A set of protocols, routines, and tools for building software applications. In the context of AI, APIs allow developers to integrate AI capabilities into their applications or access AI services provided by companies like OpenAI or Google.

Artificial intelligence A branch of computer science focused on creating systems that can perform tasks which typically require human intelligence. These tasks include learning, reasoning, problem-solving, perception, language understanding, and creativity. AI systems range from simple programs that solve specific problems to complex learning systems that adapt and operate autonomously.

Attention mechanism A key component in many modern AI models, particularly in natural language processing. It allows the model to focus on specific parts of the input data when producing an output, mimicking human attention and greatly improving the performance of tasks like translation and text summarisation.

Augmentation The enhancement of human capabilities or experiences through the use of technology, particularly artificial intelligence and other digital tools. In academic contexts, augmentation can refer to the use of AI to support and enhance research, writing, and analytical processes.

Automation/Automated The technology-enabled process of making systems or processes function automatically, without human intervention. In academia, automation can streamline repetitive tasks, allowing researchers to focus on other aspects of their work.

Autonomous systems AI systems capable of operating and making decisions without direct human control. These systems use ML algorithms to adapt to new situations and improve their performance over time.

B

Bias Systematic errors or unfairness in data, algorithms, or interpretation of results. It can manifest in various forms, including data bias, algorithmic bias, and interpretation bias. Addressing bias in AI is critical to ensure fairness, accuracy, and ethical use of technology in academic research. This involves careful data selection, algorithm design, and ongoing monitoring to identify and mitigate potential biases that could skew research outcomes or perpetuate societal inequalities.

Big Data Extremely large datasets that may be analysed to reveal patterns, trends, and associations, especially relating to human behaviour and interactions. In academia, Big Data offers unprecedented opportunities for research but also presents challenges in terms of storage, analysis, and ethical considerations.

Black Box AI AI systems whose decision-making processes are not transparent or easily interpretable by humans. This lack of explainability can be problematic in academic research, where understanding the reasoning behind conclusions is crucial.

Bodies of knowledge In the context of AI and academic research, this term refers to the vast collections of information, theories, and data. It's essentially the AI's "textbook" – a comprehensive repository of information it can draw upon to generate responses or perform tasks.

Bot Short for "robot", a bot is a software application that runs automated tasks over the internet. Bots can be used for tasks like literature searches, data collection, or even as research assistants.

C

Chatbot A software application designed to simulate conversation with human users, especially over the internet. It uses natural language processing (NLP) and artificial intelligence to understand user queries and generate responses. Chatbots can range from simple, rule-based systems that respond to specific keywords or phrases, to more advanced AI-driven bots capable of learning and adapting to user interactions over time.

ChatGPT An AI chatbot developed by OpenAI, based on the Generative Pre-trained Transformer (GPT) architecture. ChatGPT has gained significant attention in academia for its ability to engage in human-like conversations, answer questions, and assist with writing tasks.

Clustering A ML technique that involves grouping similar data points together. It's used in academic research for tasks, such as data exploration and pattern recognition.

Context window The amount of text (information) an AI can "remember" and consider when generating a response. Think of it as the AI's short-term memory or attention span.

Conversation-style chatbot A type of chatbot designed to mimic human-like conversational interactions.

Compute The amount of computational power and resources required to run AI models or perform technological tasks. The availability of compute can significantly impact the scale and complexity of AI models that can be developed and deployed.

Computational power The capacity of a computer or a system to process and manipulate data. It is typically measured by the speed and efficiency with which a system can execute instructions, handle complex calculations, or process large amounts of data. Advancements in computational power have been a key enabler for the development and deployment of sophisticated AI applications in academic research.

Computer program A sequence of instructions written to perform a specified task with a computer. These instructions provide the guidelines for how the program operates and interacts with other software and hardware.

Co-pilot A system or tool that assists users in completing tasks. In the context of AI, it refers to AI-powered assistants that work alongside humans, augmenting their capabilities.

D

Dataset A collection of data used in research and analysis. Key characteristics include: size (the number of records and features); type (e.g. numerical, categorical, textual, or a combination); structure (e.g. organised in a defined schema or unstructured); quality (accuracy, completeness, and consistency); and source (origin and collection method, which can affect reliability and relevance).

Deep learning A subset of ML based on learning data representations, as opposed to task-specific algorithms. It involves the use of large neural networks with many layers of nodes (hence "deep"), trained on vast amounts of data. These neural networks attempt to simulate the behaviour of the human brain – albeit in a limited sense – to process data and create patterns for decision making.

Deep learning architecture The structure and design of neural networks used in deep learning. These architectures are layered constructs of algorithms intended to model high-level abstractions in data.

Document analysis The use of AI tools to extract, analyse, and summarise information from academic papers, reports, or other documents. This can be particularly useful for literature reviews or data extraction from multiple sources.

Draft zero AI tools can create initial drafts of academic writing. Ideally, these drafts should be used for brainstorming and/or getting your initial thoughts on the page, and not be submitted for publication as a replacement for human contributions.

E

Ethical AI The development and use of artificial intelligence in ways that adhere to moral principles and values. For academics, this might involve considering the ethical implications of using AI tools in research, such as potential biases, privacy concerns, or the impact on human subjects.

Explainability The degree to which the internal workings or decision-making processes of an AI system can be understood and interpreted by humans. Explainability allows researchers to understand how conclusions were reached, validate results, and identify potential biases or errors. Explainable AI (XAI) refers to methods and techniques that make AI systems more transparent and interpretable, which is particularly important in fields where the reasoning behind decisions or predictions needs to be clearly articulated.

Everyday AI AI technologies and tools that have become integrated into daily academic workflows. This term encompasses the various AI-powered applications that researchers might use regularly, such as writing assistants, reference managers, or data analysis tools, which can enhance productivity and efficiency in academic work.

Expert systems A branch of artificial intelligence that emulates the decision-making ability of a human expert, designed to solve complex problems by reasoning through bodies of knowledge. In academic contexts, expert systems can assist researchers in specialised fields by providing guidance or analysis based on established knowledge in the discipline.

F

Feedback loop The iterative process of providing input to an AI system, receiving output, and then refining the input based on the output. This cycle can help in improving the relevance and accuracy of AI-generated content.

Few-shot learning An AI capability where a model can make accurate predictions based on only a few examples. This can be useful when working with limited datasets or when trying to apply AI tools to niche research areas.

Fine-tuning The process of adapting a pre-trained AI model to a specific task or domain. For academics, this could involve customising a general-purpose AI writing assistant to better understand and generate content in their specific field of study.

G

Generative AI (GenAI) AI systems capable of creating new content, such as text, images, or code. Generative AI can assist with tasks like drafting literature reviews, generating research questions, or creating visual aids for presentations.

GPT (Generative Pre-trained Transformer) A type of large language model that uses deep learning to produce human-like text. GPT models, such as those powering ChatGPT, are increasingly used by academics for tasks like writing assistance, brainstorming, and summarisation.

GPT-3 (GPT-4, etc.) Specific iterations of the GPT language model developed by OpenAI. GPT-3 was groundbreaking at the time. GPT-4 was its successor. These models power various AI tools used in academic workflows, such as writing assistants, language translation, and text summarisation. While powerful, academics should be aware of their limitations, including potential biases and the need to fact-check outputs. As new versions are released, they are likely to offer enhanced capabilities but may also present new challenges for academics.

H

Hallucinations Instances where AI models generate plausible-sounding but factually incorrect or nonsensical information. For academics using AI tools, it's crucial to be aware of this limitation and to verify AI-generated content.

Hybrid intelligence The combination of human and artificial intelligence to solve complex problems. In academic workflows, this often involves using AI tools to augment human capabilities, such as using AI for initial data analysis before applying human expertise for interpretation.

Human-in-the-loop An approach where human input (intervention and oversight) is incorporated into AI systems to improve decision-making and outcomes.

I

Intelligent machines Systems or devices that mimic human intelligence, capable of learning, problem-solving, and adapting to new situations. Intelligent machines can range from AI writing assistants to complex research tools that analyse data.

Information retrieval The process of obtaining relevant information from a large collection of data. AI-powered information retrieval systems can significantly enhance academic research by quickly identifying and extracting information from vast databases of scholarly literature.

Iterative prompting The process of refining and adjusting prompts given to AI systems to improve the quality and relevance of outputs.

Interpretability The degree to which an AI system's decision-making process can be understood by humans. For academics using AI tools, interpretability is crucial for understanding the reliability and potential biases of AI-generated outputs.

Implicit bias in AI Unintended prejudices that can be present in AI systems, often reflecting biases in training data or algorithm design. Academics should be aware of potential implicit biases when using AI tools for research or analysis to ensure fair and accurate results.

K

Knowledge base A structured collection of information that an AI system uses to generate responses or make decisions.

Keyword extraction An AI-powered process that automatically identifies and extracts the most important or frequently used words or phrases from a text. This functionality can be particularly useful for academics when summarising research papers or identifying key themes in large bodies of literature.

Knowledge graph A network representation of relationships between entities (e.g. concepts, people, events) in a knowledge domain. AI-powered knowledge graphs can help researchers visualise connections within their field of study, potentially revealing new research directions or unexplored relationships between concepts.

L

Large language models (LLMs) Advanced AI systems trained on vast amounts of text data, capable of understanding and generating human-like text. LLMs, such as GPT-3 and GPT-4, represent the AI technology underpinning many AI writing assistants and research tools used in academia.

Large neural network models Complex artificial neural networks with many layers and parameters, designed to process and analyse large amounts of data. These models underpin various AI tools used for tasks such as natural language processing, image recognition, and data analysis.

M

Machine learning A subset of AI that focuses on the development of algorithms and statistical models that enable computer systems to improve their performance on a specific task through experience. ML is used in various tools for data analysis, pattern recognition, and predictive modelling across disciplines.

Model(s) In AI, a model refers to the computational representation of a system or process, trained on data to make predictions or decisions.

Multi-modal AI systems that can process and integrate information from multiple types of input (e.g. text, images, audio). Multi-modal AI tools can be particularly useful for researchers working with diverse data types or in interdisciplinary fields.

N

Narrow AI Also known as "weak AI" or 'specialised AI', narrow AI refers to artificial intelligence systems designed to perform specific tasks within a limited domain. Unlike the sci-fi dream of general AI that can match human-level cognition across all areas, narrow AI excels at particular functions but lacks broader capabilities. Think of it as a highly skilled specialist rather than a jack-of-all-trades.

Natural language The language that humans naturally speak or write, as opposed to artificial or computer languages. In the context of AI, natural language refers to the ability of AI systems to understand and generate human language in a way that feels natural and intuitive.

Natural language processing (NLP) A branch of AI that focuses on the interaction between computers and human language. NLP enables AI systems to understand, interpret, and generate human language. NLP powers many writing assistance tools, chatbots, and research aids.

Neural network A computing system inspired by the biological neural networks in human brains. Neural networks are the foundation of many modern AI systems, including those used in academic tools for data analysis, language processing, and pattern recognition.

O

OpenAI A research organisation focused on developing AI, perhaps best known for creating ChatGPT – putting the higher education system into a spin, largely due to concerns that students would use it in ways that compromised academic integrity.

Optical Character Recognition (OCR) AI-powered technology that converts different types of documents, such as scanned paper documents, PDFs, or images, into editable and searchable data.

P

Persona A set of characteristics and behaviours assigned to an AI system to give it a distinct personality or role. Academics might use different AI personas for various tasks, such as a "research assistant" persona for literature reviews or a "writing coach" persona for manuscript editing.

Program A set of instructions that tell a computer how to perform a specific task.

Prompt An input or instruction is given to an AI system to elicit a specific response or action.

Prompt engineering The practice of designing and refining inputs to AI systems to achieve desired outputs. This skill is increasingly important for academics using AI tools, as it can significantly impact the quality and relevance of AI-generated content.

Plagiarism detection tools Tools that compare text against a large database of sources to identify potential instances of plagiarism. Please question the reliability and validity of their outputs before putting your trust in them!

R

Reinforcement learning A type of ML where an AI agent learns to make decisions by taking actions in an environment to maximise a reward.

Robustness The ability of an AI system to maintain its performance under various conditions or when faced with unexpected inputs.

For academics, considering the robustness of AI tools is important when relying on them for critical research tasks.

S

Semantic (search) A search method that attempts to understand the intent and contextual meaning of search queries, rather than just matching keywords.

Sentiment analysis AI techniques used to determine the emotional tone behind words. This can be useful in analysing large text datasets.

Singularity A hypothetical future point at which artificial intelligence surpasses human intelligence.

Strong AI Also known as "artificial general intelligence" (AGI), strong AI refers to hypothetical AI systems capable of human-like general intelligence, having the ability to understand, learn, and apply intelligence across a wide range of domains. It's a concept that remains largely theoretical and is a subject of ongoing research and debate.

Supervised Learning A type of ML where the algorithm is trained on a labelled dataset.

Systems (AI Systems) Integrated sets of AI technologies designed to perform complex tasks or solve specific problems.

T

Training data The dataset used to teach an AI model how to perform its task. Understanding the nature of training data can help academics critically evaluate the potential biases or limitations of AI tools.

Turing Test A test of a machine's ability to exhibit intelligent behaviour equivalent to, or indistinguishable from, that of a human.

U

Unsupervised Learning A type of ML where the algorithm tries to find patterns in unlabelled data. This concept is relevant for academics working with exploratory data analysis or trying to discover hidden patterns in large datasets.

V

Vectorisation The process of converting text into numerical vectors that can be processed by ML algorithms. This underlies many AI-based text analysis tools used in academic research.

W

Word embedding A technique in NLP where words or phrases are mapped to vectors of real numbers. This underlies many advanced text analysis tools used in academic research.

X

XAI (Explainable AI) AI systems designed to be interpretable and understandable by humans.

Z

Zero-shot learning The ability of an AI model to solve tasks it wasn't explicitly trained on.

For Product Safety Concerns and Information please contact our EU representative GPSR@taylorandfrancis.com
Taylor & Francis Verlag GmbH, Kaufingerstraße 24, 80331 München, Germany

www.ingramcontent.com/pod-product-compliance
Lightning Source LLC
Chambersburg PA
CBHW070959050326
40689CB00014B/3419

* 9 7 8 1 0 3 2 6 6 5 2 6 9 *